GIRLS
UNINTERRUPTED

DISCARD

About the Author

Tanith Carey writes books which aim to lucidly set out the more pressing challenges for today's parents – and set out achievable strategies for how to tackle them. Her previous book, *Taming the Tiger Parent: How to Put your Child's Well-being First in a Competitive World* has been called 'a critique to re-orientate parenting' by Steve Biddulph. As an award-winning journalist, Tanith writes for a range of publications including the *Guardian*, the *Daily Telegraph*, *The Sunday Times*, the *Daily Mail* and the *Huffington Post*. This is her seventh book.

GIRLS
UNINTERRUPTED

STEPS FOR BUILDING STRONGER GIRLS
IN A CHALLENGING WORLD

TANITH CAREY

ICON

Published in the UK in 2015 by
Icon Books Ltd, Omnibus Business Centre,
39–41 North Road, London N7 9DP
email: info@iconbooks.com
www.iconbooks.com

Sold in the UK, Europe and Asia
by Faber & Faber Ltd, Bloomsbury House,
74–77 Great Russell Street,
London WC1B 3DA or their agents

Distributed in the UK, Europe and Asia
by TBS Ltd, TBS Distribution Centre, Colchester Road,
Frating Green, Colchester CO7 7DW

Distributed in Australia and New Zealand
by Allen & Unwin Pty Ltd,
PO Box 8500, 83 Alexander Street,
Crows Nest, NSW 2065

Distributed in South Africa by
Jonathan Ball, Office B4, The District,
41 Sir Lowry Road, Woodstock 7925

Distributed to the trade in the USA
by Consortium Book Sales and Distribution,
The Keg House, 34 Thirteenth Avenue NE, Suite 101,
Minneapolis, MN 55413-1007

Distributed in India by Penguin Books India,
7th Floor, Infinity Tower – C, DLF Cyber City,
Gurgaon 122002, Haryana

ISBN: 978-184831-820-5

An earlier edition of this book was published under the title
Where Has My Little Girl Gone? by Lion Hudson in 2011.

Text copyright © 2015 Tanith Carey

Typeset in Joanna by Marie Doherty

Printed and bound in the UK by Clays Ltd, St Ives plc

For my daughters, and yours.

CONTENTS

INTRODUCTION

When I chat to my two daughters, thirteen-year-old Lily and ten-year-old Clio, we cover all the usual topics: how their school day went, what's for dinner, why can't we get Honey, our dog, to behave.

But throughout the course of our conversations, lots of other, slightly trickier subjects also crop up, like: why is Miley Cyrus naked in her latest video, but for a pair of Dr Martens? 'I mean, I get why she's sitting on a wrecking ball,' Clio has said, 'because that's what she's singing about. But why she doesn't she have any clothes on?' From time to time, Lily has also wondered why every year at her primary school fair there is a 'beauty' tent for girls to get their nails manicured, when boys never have to bother about how they look.

So was I pleased when, the other day, Clio asked me why Rapunzel just didn't cut off her own hair and make it into a rope to get down from the tower, instead of waiting for a prince? Am I delighted that Lily's favourite game as we wait in tube stations is 'spot the model whose been airbrushed'? Frankly, yes.

Does it make me a humourless, ball-breaking man-hater? Am I brainwashing my poor little girls with politically correct feminist theory? Some people might think that. But I believe I am simply encouraging my girls to open their eyes to a world which might otherwise give them deeply unhelpful messages about who they are, and how they should feel about themselves.

My daughters are not weak and defenceless – and neither are yours. But in a world where many pubescent girls say they are more worried about getting fat than their parents dying or the outbreak of nuclear war, my view is that our daughters need help to work out why so many of their gender think this way – so they don't end up thinking like that too. They need to know that, in the words of the late Anita Roddick, there are over 3 billion women who don't look supermodels and eight who do. Because if our daughters are allowed to believe what they see all around them, they will be fooled into believing they have failed before they've even begun.

It is the best of times and the worst of times for our daughters. On one hand they have never been healthier, better educated or enjoyed more opportunities in the workplace. When I was born in 1967, women were already making huge strides towards equality. The arrival of the pill meant women finally had a choice about when or whether they wanted to have babies. The stereotypes of females as ditzy airheads, sex objects or housewives whose main job was to serve husbands was starting, finally, to crumble. In their place stood 'woman' as she had never been allowed to be: every bit as strong, capable and intelligent as a male. So by rights, my daughter Lily, born 34 years after me in 2001, should be growing up in a world where women are enjoying the benefits of that radical shift.

When I held my baby girl in my arms for first time, I really believed she had been born into a world of endless possibilities, where being a female would never hold her back.

But, already, there were hints that that promise had failed to turn into reality. With the benefit of hindsight, I now see that by the time I became a mother, there were already the first signs that the progress we had taken for granted was starting to go off the rails.

By the early 2000s, the fact that a woman could choose to

wear anything she liked was becoming twisted into the idea that in order to appear truly confident it was best to wear virtually nothing at all. Women stripped thinking it made them powerful, only to find that, far from getting respect, their willingness to liberate themselves from their clothing was turned back against them in lads' mags and music videos. Sex tapes which once ruined careers now created them, perpetuating the idea that sex was a quick way to buy legitimate celebrity and make money. Brazilian waxes to strip adult women as naked as little girls, and which also mimicked the hairlessness of females in porn, had started to be seen as 'empowering'. Yet, as questionable as I personally felt these decisions were, at least these were adult women, making adult choices.

But when little girls started to get sucked in by this undercurrent, and began judging themselves by adults' sexual standards fashioned by porn, a whole new set of previously unseen and extremely toxic effects started to emerge.

To be honest, before I wrote the first version of this book on the creeping effects of this culture on our daughters, Lily was seven and I was in shock. Like many parents, I initially believed that if I pressed enough towels to the door I could keep those toxic fumes of early sexualisation out of my home. But then one day Lily came back from primary school and told me some of her playmates had been calling each other fat in the playground and that, as a result, she and her friends had been swapping diet tips. Then a few weeks later Clio, then four, came home from a school dance club, singing that she had 'gloss on my lips and a man on my hips'. It seemed her dance teacher had not thought to question if it was a good idea to devise a 'bootylicious' routine set to the Beyoncé song 'Single Ladies' for a group of nursery age children. It was then I knew I couldn't stop the fumes, because they were already in the air my girls were breathing.

So I realised that if they were to stand a chance of growing up strong, I couldn't hide them from these things. Instead, I'd have to raise them in such a way that they could manage and filter these messages themselves.

When I talked about how to do this in the last edition of this book, there were some voices asking what all the fuss was about. One sociologist on 'Woman's Hour' demanded to know why I was denying my girls the right to their sexuality. In fact I was helping them push back against a culture which was defining their sexuality before they had a chance to define it for themselves.

'Moral panic' is a phrase I often hear wheeled out to silence concerns about how girls are affected by these messages. But is it really prudish or panicky to ask that our children enjoy uninterrupted childhoods where they are not beset by self-consciousness about how they look as soon as they are old enough to recognise themselves in the mirror?

Modern life – and the way we adults express ourselves in it – may be evolving at a breakneck speed, but our daughters still need to go through the same developmental milestones in the same order as they always have to become emotionally healthy adults. Just because a child has the opportunity to dress up like a grown-up on the outside, doesn't mean she is ready to be treated the same way on the inside.

My girls, and yours, probably see more images of physical beauty in one month than we saw in our entire childhoods. They are growing up in a world where their worth is measured by how closely they match those ideals. No matter what's going on in their brains, beauty has become an obligation. Yet even if they achieve those ideals, it's never enough. Girls today are caught in a double bind. If they fail in this beauty contest they are made to feel like they don't count. If they succeed, 'pretty' becomes all that they are.

As a parenting writer with a wide-ranging remit to investigate the ongoing effects of these developments on our children, I have been in a privileged position to see how the situation is evolving. From this vantage point, I have not only seen how sustained this assault is, I have also seen how fast-moving it has become. When I originally wrote on the subject, sexting was almost unheard of. Now the latest research says teens accept it as a way of life. Self-harm, scarcely known in schools a few years ago, has soared – there has been a 41 per cent increase in calls from children to their helpline about self-harm over the last year alone, according to Childline.

But self-harm has not just ripped through our classrooms in the form of cutting. Virus-like, the internet has enabled it to morph into the new phenomenon of cyber self-harm, where children post hurtful comments about themselves in order to attract strangers to troll them and help put their self-loathing into words. When I last assessed the situation, size eight was the Holy Grail of thinness. Now it's size zero. 'Thinspiration' and thigh gaps have also become aspirational, making our girls believe they should disappear, quite literally, into thin air before they've even grown into their bodies in the first place.

Then of course there has been the evolution of pornography. Naturally, it's porn's job to be graphic. That's the whole point. What was surprising a few years ago was how easily accessible it was to anyone, of any age, who could type the word 'sex' into Google. What's surprising now is how much more violent and degrading porn is becoming in order to maintain the novelty factor.

The pace of these changes, powered by a constantly evolving internet, is so fast, we can't simply firefight one crisis after another. Instead, as parents, we need to be a firm centre in the middle of this storm. That's why this book takes a three-pronged approach.

So that we start off from the best possible position to protect our girls, the first section deals with how to organise our own attitudes and ideas, so that the conscious, and unconscious, messages we send to our girls are healthy, clear and consistent.

The second part looks at how, by building self-worth in our children, we can go some way towards inoculating them. If we can create a strong core of self-belief in our girls' formative years, they will be better able to stand firm against the pressure to reduce them to nothing more than their physical beauty. By really opening up channels of communication in the tween years, we have a chance of staying closer to them when the going really gets tough. The good news is that the latest research shows the best defence against bad influences is you, the parent. One upside of the sexualised culture is that fewer topics are off limits when we talk to our children – and there really are age-appropriate ways to tackle every subject, from sexting to STDs.

The third section looks at the world through the eyes of our children. It looks at how they see it – and how we need to teach them to discover for themselves how to discern what's good and bad. From sexting to self-harm, from phone addiction to friendship problems, this part will look at the most common challenges parents face when trying to keep their girls strong. It will help you comprehend those challenges so you are in the best position to understand them. Then it gives you the practical tools to help you and your daughter push back. It will offer dozens of achievable ways you can help to tone down, if not turn off, the effects of 'raunch culture'.

For the sake of our girls, we can't forget about the well-being of boys. They are their future friends, boyfriends and husbands, after all. Just because girls were the first in the firing line doesn't mean that our sons aren't suffering too. Boys are also pressured to behave in the macho ways they see displayed in pop, porn and video games. They are fast creeping up on girls in terms of how much they worry about their appearance. They are expressing their need to conform to stereotypes with 'bigorexia' – the need to bulk up to look buff. They are also often miserable because they are struggling to connect with girls the way they'd like to. In the same way that we are talking about femininity, boys also need a chance to talk about masculinity. Ultimately our goal should be for both sexes to have dignity during their childhoods.

But until that happens, we need to help our children become strong and insightful enough to wage that campaign. As a mother of girls, my focus in this book is on my daughters, but there are still plenty more books to be written by fathers of sons, to make boys just as self-aware.

None of this can happen overnight. The sooner we begin, the better. The tween years – the ages between seven and twelve – offer a critical window when parents can help girls develop an unassailable sense of self. It's during this period that our power to positively influence our children is also at its peak – before the inevitable separation of adolescence means our daughters' peers begin to drown us out. If we really work at staying connected to our girls in those years, we have a better chance of being able to guide them when life becomes more challenging.

Our society won't stop sending these destructive messages. But by becoming aware, we can filter the air around our children so they can breathe deeply and grow stronger.

Don't see helping girls reject these negative messages as one more job to add to your already packed to-do list. By becoming a conscious parent, by talking more and providing daily subtitles to help your child to understand life, you will communicate better and the conversations you have will be livelier and more invigorating.

Your bond will be stronger. Your girl's knowledge of herself will be deeper and her respect for you will be more profound.

The younger you start, the stronger the roots she will have to grow sturdy enough to resist the temptation to degrade or sacrifice any part of herself when the pressure piles on in her teenage years. But all is not lost if we miss that window. Just by becoming a more aware parent today, you can help make your daughter more media-aware and emotionally literate. In the two minutes you take to show her how a magazine photograph of an ultra-skinny perfect model has been airbrushed, you have taught her not to hold herself up to an image of perfection that doesn't exist. By talking about and explaining what's happening around her today, you can shelter her against the *drip, drip, drip* erosion of her self-worth. That's why this book offers many suggestions for parents of girls of all ages. With the best will in the world, it would be impossible to put them all into practice. As you know your daughter best, you need to pick the most appropriate ones for you and your family.

Parts of this book will be upsetting. Facing up to what's out there – and making our girls more resilient and robust – isn't going to be easy. You may even have to come back to the sections meant for older girls if they are too much for now. As you read, you may also have to question if the creeping sexualisation of society has affected your values too. You may have to ask yourself if you have unknowingly added to the pressure by joining in the push to make our daughters the brightest and the best. But if all this helps your girl to be a little more true to herself – rather than feel she has to fit into today's stifling stereotypes of 'sexiness', beauty and perfection – then you will have won back her freedom to live without these restraints and develop at her own pace.

If we don't face up to it, the price is high. When girls wander through life thinking there is something wrong with them it makes them feel anxious, lost and powerless. Unsure of how to make themselves feel whole, too many try to fill this emptiness with fixes like diets, meaningless sex, self-harm, oblivion drinking and drugs. The problem is that because these influences are inundating them at such critical times in their lives, these wounds don't always heal, and without being shown how to fill this void, they will carry these insecurities into their adult lives.

Public Health England says that one in ten children now has a mental health issue, and a third of teenagers feel 'low, sad or down' at least once a week. According to the All Party Parliamentary Group on Body Image: 'One in four seven-year-old girls have tried to lose weight at least once.' More than a quarter of children say they 'often feel depressed' – and the thing that makes girls most unhappy is how they look. It's heartbreaking that as early as nine and ten, our daughters are already judging themselves as losers in the beauty contest of life.

One of the most insidious and least recognised effects is that our girls are also losing their voices. By the time they are ten, 13 per cent of girls aged ten to seventeen would avoid giving an opinion. The reason? They don't want to draw attention to themselves because of the way they look.

As a mother of two girls myself, I wrote this book because I do not want my children, with all their accomplishments and wonders, to be judged solely on appearance – and to feel silenced when they want to talk back and defend themselves. I do not want them to be exposed at every turn to a hyper-sexualised culture where sex is only a commodity and women are rated mainly on how 'hot' they are, or most of their headspace gets used up trying to work out what's wrong with them, when they are more than good enough as it is. My daughters don't deserve to feel like this – and neither do yours.

PART ONE

Building a Strong Foundation

US AS PARENTS

'Mum and dad, can I have a nose job please?'

It's just after 10am in Harley Street, and the doors have opened at one of the capital's larger plastic surgery clinics. At the reception, patients are being greeted by a rank of identikit receptionists in black suits and red lipstick, like the all-girl rock band in the 'Addicted to Love' video. Now dotted around the beige upholstery, the first intake of customers is busy leafing through a stack of celebrity magazines. My job this morning is to ask them why they are here. After all, the number of people undergoing plastic surgery in the UK is rising at the fastest rate in history. So why exactly has this need to look perfect become such an epidemic – and how, at a time of economic hardship and high unemployment, do people find the money?

Because my brief was just that, I had no other expectations. But as the waiting room began to fill, it was striking to see that so many of the women here were in their late teens or early twenties.

Flawlessly made up and doe-eyed, Amelie has the petite face and body of a young Audrey Hepburn – and the pert boobs, outlined in a skin-tight T-shirt, of a glamour model. In fact, she works as a cosmetics sales assistant in a nearby department store, and she is back for a post-operative review after getting her 32B boobs boosted two cup sizes 'for confidence'.

The £4,500 cost of the operation is probably not far off a quarter of her yearly take-home salary. But, like so many of her generation who can't afford to move out, Amelie lives at home – and anyway her mum and dad paid for the surgery.

'I told them I wanted them done and they said: "OK, if that's what you want."' she explains matter-of-factly, as if her parents were paying the down-payment on her first car. 'They didn't worry. They said: "If it makes you feel better about yourself, then that's fine."'

In the other corner of the room, I approach Elaine, 20. With her tongue stud and skinny jeans, Elaine looks like more like an off-duty member of a girl-band than the legal secretary she is. She recently had a nose job, once again paid for in part by a loan from the bank of mum and dad.

'I know it's going to sound really funny, but there was nothing wrong with my old nose,' she insists. 'It just looked a bit funny in pictures. My friend had it done when she was eighteen. Plus everyone's doing it. Surgery is getting younger these days. Six of my friends have had boob jobs. One went up to a double F and she loves all the men paying her attention. As soon as you find out from your friends that it doesn't hurt that much, there's nothing to stop you. The moment I woke up from my nose job, I asked about a boob job. I am still thinking about it.'

Because it's her first session, Courtney, eighteen, is being accompanied by her mother this morning. They have travelled from Kent to start a course of £1,200 laser treatments to get rid of Courtney's stretch marks. Again, flawlessly made up to airbrush standards – and a size six in skinny jeans and a T-shirt which is cutaway to reveal her tiny waist – Courtney continually smoothes down her waterfall of glossy auburn hair.

As if she is about to being cured of a life-threatening disease, Courtney explains that she developed 'terrible red lines' across her stomach and thighs when she put on two stone after starting the contraceptive pill. Now, with just a few months to go before the start of a performing arts course, both mum and daughter are frantically trying to get rid of them for fear they should stand in the way of her career.

Once she's gone in for her treatment, mum Justine confides why, as a responsible parent, she felt she had no choice but to do something. 'It's true the treatments are quite expensive. But what choice have you got when something like this is ruining your daughter's life? It's wrecked her social life. When her friends ring her and ask her to join them on sleepovers, she says no because she can't bear anyone to see her in her underwear.'

'I saw her sitting there with the tears streaming down her face. It was heartbreaking. She kept saying: "Why has this happened to me, Mum? How could this happen to me?"'

University student Louise is also here courtesy of her parents' generosity, although with only the tiniest bump on her nose, it's hard to foresee how her life will change post-rhinoplasty. But her elder sister had already been treated to surgery by their parents to tidy up some loose skin after losing weight, and, so that they were absolutely fair, her parents told Louise that she could think of something to have done too.

It was just a snapshot. But as I interviewed more girls during my research for this book, I found almost every young woman has a notional shopping list of some fault she feels has to get 'fixed'. Indeed, a study by Girlguiding UK found that 12 per cent of 16- to 21-year-olds would consider cosmetic surgery. The result is that market researchers now consider young people the prime plastic surgery growth market. In recent years, Mintel has found that it's the number of young people considering cosmetic surgery that has gone up most sharply. Almost six in ten 16- to 24-year-olds – young people in the prime of their looks and attractiveness – want surgery to improve or 'correct' their looks.

The only thing that stands in their way is money – but with parents increasingly willing to foot the bill, that's becoming less of a barrier to 'fixing' what they believe is wrong with them.

Of course, it's painful for any parent to witness the anxieties teenage girls go through about their looks. But what was sobering was the quality of the reasons these young women had for going under the knife. As I remembered, plastic surgery used to be undertaken to fix flaws that caused crippling insecurities and unhappiness. Yet the main explanations I heard that day were that their friends had had something done too, they wanted to look better in pictures – or just because they could.

Today, such treatments are seen as quick, easy and less invasive – with women feeling that if they are out there, it's their obligation to use them to fit into today's beauty standards. None of the women in the waiting room cited celebrity culture. But then it's so pervasive and ingrained that most girls grow up never having known any other ideal but perfection. Most learned about makeovers from TV shows at their mothers' knees.

But far from trying to talk their girls out of it, or attempting to put these concerns into perspective, what surprised me was how many parents were prepared to foot the bill. Whatever objections they raised in private or in the run-up to the operations – which I was not privy to – they still handed over their credit cards.

Like mentors on *The X Factor*, in the final analysis they went along with the belief that cosmetic enhancement – and a perfect cookie-cutter appearance – is what a modern girl needs to get on in life.

For even younger girls, the trend is echoed in the rise in the child beauty industry. Ten years ago, there were virtually no mini beauty contests in Britain. While the French Government has now moved to outlaw them, there are now more than 30 in the UK, thanks, in part, to the instant fame bestowed by reality television programmes like *Toddlers and Tiaras*.

More than 12,000 girls are entered into the Miss Teen Queen UK pageant every year alone. Yet none of this would be happening without the parenting drive and cash to make it happen. As Cheryl, a mother I interviewed after she proudly paid for not one, but two of her daughters to have boob jobs the moment they turned eighteen, told me: 'To me, [the operations] are the best things the girls have ever done.'

Rather than question the culture that made her girls sob into their pillows every night because they saw themselves as 'flat-chested', Cheryl, 49, insisted: 'I think it shows I'm a better parent. After they had the op, it was like watching two flowers unfurl.'

Far from curing this restlessness about their appearance, it seems that fixing one perceived flaw just leads girls to worry about another. Before the wedding of Cheryl's older daughter a few years later, perhaps it should not have been a surprise to hear that the bride-to-be prepared for her big day by getting her lips plumped and her Botox done, despite being barely in her twenties.

It would be unfair to single out any one mother too much. Despite how some of our values are affecting our daughters, we parents are responding to the influences around us. Most mothers genuinely believe they are doing their best to help their girls get on in life.

This attitude that girls need constant improvement is even catching on in primary schools, the one bastion where we might hope learning is prioritised over looks. Yet over the last five years, prom nights have become *de rigueur* for children as young as seven, and proud mums and dads don't hesitate to fork out small fortunes on make-up artists, Barbie-doll dresses and limos. Indeed, when I wrote my last book on girls, most weeks there were stories in the papers of mums putting put six-year-old children on strict calorie-controlled diets, bleaching their teeth and signing them up for pole-dancing lessons, lest they lose out in life.

The stories which hit the headlines were, of course, extreme examples that few parents reading this would identify with. Yet, though the manner and style of presentation might vary, this is a tendency filtering through all sections of society. They may be less newsworthy, but I've known mothers at the nation's most exclusive schools who talk proudly about how they paid to have their thirteen-year-old daughter's teeth veneered to give them a 'Hollywood smile', or how they took them to a top salon to get £250 highlights because their daughter's 'mousy' brown locks 'didn't make them stand out'.

But just as I had to look deeper at my own values, and examine whether my best intentioned references to 'healthy foods' and my regular gym sessions had made my daughter Lily start to believe that it's part of a female's job description to fret about her body, it helps to go back to the source.

Take yourself back to the moment you knew you were having a baby girl. Was your first thought to imagine how pretty she was going to be, or the lovely dresses you were going to put her in? If you're also the parent of a boy, ask yourself if you felt something similar when you learned you were having a son. Would it be fair to say that his outfits and how handsome he might be were lower on your list of initial concerns? It's a tough thing to admit, but if we are going to fight against our girls being judged on how they look, we have to start by examining our own expectations – and how they have been shaped in us over the last twenty or 30 years.

After all, if we were born during or after the sixties, we were the first generation to grow up in a world dominated by television. As TV became our main national pastime, as children we quickly picked up that, for a woman, being thin and beautiful equals being sexy and successful.

In our lifetimes, we saw the explosion of reality stars, WAGs and manufactured girl bands who have sent the lesson that you can be rich and famous without talent. Pretty and pushy is all you need. The fact is that as mothers we have been under siege too. We have also been affected by the media messages which tell us that we can never be beautiful or thin enough. As these celebrities have racked up continuous attention and impressive wealth – and reality TV has made this feel within the grasp of everybody – have we not also signed up to the idea that females needs to look a certain way to get on in life?

Even as grown women, we may never have known the peace of feeling good about our bodies. As I write, a record-breaking two out of three women have tried to lose weight in the past year – up from 63 per cent the previous year to an all-time high of 65 per cent, according to Mintel. Without realising it, have we also come to covet a celebrity lifestyle and appearance for our own children and equate beauty and thinness with power?

Of course, through the ages, parents have always prized their daughters' attractiveness. Because the faces of our children – their smooth skin, shiny hair, large eyes and soft features – are the prototype for adult perfection, little girls are, by their very nature, beautiful. This is such a difficult area for parents, because we are damned if we do address appearance with our girls, and damned if we don't. We can't pretend that looks don't matter one bit. The acute sensitivity of girls on this topic is such that those with parents who never mention it assume it's because they are ugly. So simply not attaching any importance to appearance whatsoever is not the answer.

However, it's how much importance we attach to looks in a society already obsessed by looks – where everyone is measured on a sliding scale of perfection – that is now key. So while we should feel free to acknowledge beauty, we have to be even more careful that we try not to fall in with the trend of making it the most important quality about our girls. We need to make it clear that their beauty is a small part of what they are – not who they are.

Starting early in their lives, it's vital to prize other values – like kindness, honesty, generosity, self-awareness and self-acceptance – that often get drowned out in a culture of superficiality. Rather than encourage the draw towards celebrity and consumerism, we need to try to divert them away from the identikit ideal of feminine attractiveness – perma-tanned skin, hair that will only pass muster if it's glossy enough for a shampoo ad and a lithe, fat-free body – towards qualities which are not visible. If, as their most important role models, we endorse society's message that looks are the most important thing about them, we don't equip our children for success. We set them up for a lifetime of disappointment.

Why parents feel powerless

Being a parent of girls is a tough job. But it's even tougher for the families of today who are trying to screen out so many more negative influences on their daughters' healthy development. Compare, for a moment, the influences on your own childhood, with those on your daughter's.

Probably, during your childhood, if you watched TV alone, it was mainly in the prescribed after-school period, or on Saturday morning when there were shows created for kids your age.

Certainly when I was growing up in the Seventies, there was just one TV, and the whole family would gather round to watch variety programmes designed for everyone, like *This is Your Life* or *The Morecambe and Wise Show*. True, there was sexism, much of it a spill-over from the *Carry On* humour of the Sixties. Sometimes, the TV showed women as passive sex objects, like in *Miss World*. But still, the only place you could be guaranteed to see a topless woman was not on TV, but on page three of the *Sun*.

Though it may have been implied, there wasn't nearly as much sex in our media – and certainly nothing of the intensity we have now. Anything much stronger than a kiss or a mild swear word was unheard of before the 9pm watershed, which was rigorously policed. Compared with children growing up today, our childhoods were androgynous.

Because it's all happened relatively quickly, it's hard for us as parents to take on what our daughters' childhoods are really like, and how the world looks from their point of view. With sexuality and body image now so deeply woven into music, advertising, TV, magazines, fashion and the internet they face, it's understandable that many parents already feel defeated. They feel society has moved on and that it's a fact of life they have to live with.

When I first wrote about this three years ago, the families I spoke to handled creeping sexualisation in a variety of ways. Generally, they sat on a sliding scale between prohibitive – believing they could screen it all out – and permissive – thinking they had no choice but to go along with it. In the period since then, I have noticed that we are not as shocked anymore. That, worryingly, we have come to accept aspects of sexualisation, like girls of eight looking and acting like teens, without question. It is on the way to becoming normal. So, before we start looking at where we need to go from here, it may be worthwhile to look at where we, as parents, are starting from. While the range of viewpoints that follow may not be a definitive list, look through to see if any of these preconceptions match your own:

■■■■■ 'There's nothing we can do – so why try?'

Among the many parents I interviewed for this book, there was a real sense of fear and powerlessness. Many had taken the route of weary surrender. 'There's nothing we can do' was a common refrain. Indeed some have already given up or accepted growing up sooner as the status quo.

Mothers and fathers told me they didn't know where to start because the internet and the media felt too vast and out of control. Everything was moving too fast. These are parents who feel drowned out as advertisers, retailers, programmers, video makers and negative peer pressure ride roughshod over their influence.

According to a survey of 1,000 parents of children aged under eighteen, one in five parents feel they have little or no control over what their children see on the web anymore, and a quarter feel they have lost control over what their children do on social networking sites.

The parents in this category often start off being restrictive but lose hope when they start to believe they are fighting a battle on too many fronts. Indeed a report by the British Board of Film Classification found that, by the time their children were fifteen, most parents believed it was 'game over' and that kids were so tech-savvy they could no longer control their child's viewing in any way.

But it's far too soon – and far too dangerous – to fall into a state of paralysis. While it's true that we can't shield our children, we can inoculate them from the effects by decoding – in an age appropriate way – what is happening all around them. By helping girls to question the pressures placed on them, we really can help them work out for themselves what is good and bad for them. Furthermore, far from being impotent, parent power is still a force to be reckoned with. While responsible corporations do like profits, they also hate bad publicity. Deep down, I still believe society knows it has a responsibility to collectively look after our children. So we need to ask why the vast social networks, making billions in advertising, don't have the moderators to monitor or act on the cyberbullying, trolling or images of violence and cruelty that run riot on their sites.

It took just one mother of two, Nikola Evans, to get Asda to apologise for and withdraw a display of padded bras for girls as young as nine from an aisle at their Sheffield store. Following a national outcry from parents and campaigners, Primark removed padded bras for seven year olds from its shelves, while Tesco also stopped selling 'toy' pole-dancing kits.

Advertising, TV and other forms of media also have complaints bodies – but they are, all too often, woefully underused. Remember, all it usually takes is a single complaint to launch an investigation and move society an inch closer to being more conscious and accountable for the welfare of our girls.

■■■■■ 'If I just say no, it won't happen to my child.'

Early in our daughters' childhoods, when they are still babies and toddlers, it's reassuring to tell ourselves that if we don't buy them Bratz dolls, park them in front of the internet or computer games for hours or dress them in T-shirts with slogans like 'So many boys, so little time', we can protect them from negative messages that damage their well-being. But these influences are not a tap you switch off. They are in the air they breathe, and as your child gets older, peer pressure will play an increasingly large part in the decisions your daughter makes.

If we simply try to prevent our girls from ever seeing or hearing negative messages, they will never get the chance to work out for themselves how either to spot – or to cope with – the dangers. We also risk them becoming so intrigued by the forbidden that, once they are out of our control, they become eager to try everything we've tried to keep them away from. Most of all what children need is to learn to judge for themselves.

Ultimately, it's more realistic to equip your child and warn her what's coming. Explain where the pressures come from and the commercial realities behind them. Explain that marketers target young girls because they are the most naïve consumers, and that the ads only work by playing on girls' insecurities and desire to fit in. Make it an ongoing conversation, and help her to see the bigger picture. By decoding what is going on around her as she experiences it, you will help her reject these messages.

■■■■■■ 'I don't want to tell her anything because
it will take away her innocence.'

Many parents also feel understandably confused and panicky about how much information to give to prepare their children. They feel afraid of robbing their daughters of their innocence by telling them of the pressures they might come under.

As parents, so many of us find it painful to acknowledge when our girls are ready to start learning more about sex. I spoke to many mums who couldn't bear the thought of sex education classes, even in Year Six, because they believed there was no need. But the risk is that if we don't tell children about sex, then the internet will get in there first – and sooner than we think. If our girls do end up learning about sex – as so many do – by stumbling across pornography before they've even had their first kiss, this is going to be as far away from the healthy messages you want to give them as possible.

Talking to your children about sex won't encourage them to go and do it. Quite the opposite. More than 250 studies have found that the best way to protect girls against early sexual behaviour is for them to be responsibly informed about sex in the first place.

Frightening though this may feel, there really are always warm, non-scary, age-appropriate ways to talk about everything. But don't keep steeling yourself to launch into the big 'birds and the bees' chat that never quite happens. Make it an ongoing dialogue with your daughter, and add more detail as and when she needs it. Let her know that sex should have context and meaning. As parents, we need to accept that it's a conversation that may feel strange to start off with. But it's better to accept what's happening, because it will happen whether we want it to or not. Once you get going, you may even warm to the subject – although don't tell her more than she needs, you will end up confusing her. In the final event, you won't be with your daughter when she makes her sexual choices – but if you've talked her through them, she's likely to choose the safer, more meaningful options.

■■■■ 'My daughter's a good girl. She's not interested.'

This was a common refrain. In fact, very few parents I spoke to – even those with older girls – were aware of their children seeing sexual content like pornography as anything other than a one-off or completely by accident. The fact that girls are excellent secret keepers helps parents live in this bubble.

Among the many studies to paint a rather different picture is a report by LSE which found that while 57 per cent of children between the ages of nine and nineteen have seen porn, only 16 per cent of their parents knew. When it comes to knowing whether or not their daughters are having sex, parents are also wide of the mark. Studies have found that in 50 per cent of cases, mums and dads who believed their children were virgins were wrong.

So be realistic. Difficult though it can be to face up to, you'll be in a stronger position if you accept your children as sexual beings, than if you avoid the uncomfortable truth that they are.

■■■■ 'Everyone else's kids are doing it – so I can't stop mine.'

Many parents feel that however much they protect their girls, they will just hear it all from their peers at school anyway, so what's the point? Others say they don't speak up because other parents aren't saying much either, so that probably means it's OK.

Underlying this is also the worry that they won't look 'cool' if they are the only ones who don't let their daughters sign up to social networks or see films that are rated for an older audience.

But just as you would hope your child would stand up to peer group pressure, it's important you do the same. Make your own decisions. It takes a strong parent to say no when most of the others are saying yes. I know of one mother who vetoed a plan by a group of other mothers to have a 'makeover tent' at their primary school fête. She says they now ignore her, but she's impervious because she truly believes she did the right thing for her nine-year-old daughter.

When it comes to going against other parents, what's more important? The fact that, at worst, you might be viewed as the killjoy at the school gates, or protecting your child and possibly helping other parents be more conscious about the messages they are sending out?

Don't let other parents decide on how fast your child grows up just because you don't want to stick out. Apart from anything else, you will also be setting a good example to your daughter by standing up for what you believe in.

■■■■■ 'It's just the way kids are nowadays.'

Tellingly, I didn't include this justification in the first version of this book because parents were still only just waking up to the advancing pace of sexualisation. But three years down the line accelerated childhood is rapidly on the way to becoming the norm.

To counter this, we need to keep reminding ourselves that a child's brain and emotional development are on the same timetable that they have been on for tens of thousands of years – and these stages cannot be rushed, no matter what. If we start to accept that 'it's just the way kids are', are we also prepared to accept the commensurate rise in mental health disorders? Are we prepared to accept that a state of affairs where, despite all their brain power and potential, more girls say they want to be thin than win the Nobel Peace Prize?

We are the last generation who enjoyed a less self-conscious, more carefree type of childhood, freer from worries about looks. Rather than giving in and accepting that our girls won't get that solid grounding, don't we owe it to them to hold the line?

■■■■■ 'I don't think it's such a bad thing.'

Some parents actively enjoy the fact that their children grow up fast. They see it as a sign that their children are more sophisticated and desirable, and as a reflection of their own ability to move with the times.

Increasingly, many also believe it makes them look like cooler parents, and enjoy the popularity that comes with being the more permissive grown-ups among their child's circle.

Mums who think they married well due to their own good looks – or who feel insecure about the lack of them – may also find it flattering and amusing to hear their daughters called 'hot' as early as ten or eleven, and are happy to share the credit. This is partly because, more than ever, beauty is seen as the way to get ahead.

For these parents, their own adolescence may be instructing them subconsciously. They may be the parents who attracted notoriety at school by being the first to lose their virginity or drink alcohol. Conversely, they may have felt ignored or slighted by the opposite sex at the same age, and not want the same thing to happen to their girls. But children are not horses to be set in a race to sexual competency, and they are living their childhoods, not yours. We can't live through them to make up for what we feel we missed out on, or to emulate what we think we gained. Ask yourself – what exactly is the rush? Trying too hard to be adult can only distract during a crucial window in the education and development of our girls. They have the rest of their lives for that. And just because your daughter looks grown-up and 'sexy', doesn't mean she is inside. She is more exposed than you think.

■■■■ 'We did it all in my day.'

Other parents dismiss sexualisation by saying every generation is shocked by what the younger generation does. 'We did all that in our day,' they say. 'We went out with boys and drank and smoked – and we turned out OK, didn't we?'

These parents argue that little girls have always wanted to look older – or that they tried on their mums' high heels, and it didn't do them any harm. That is perfectly true, but the stakes have got so much higher. While we may remember rolling up our skirts the moment the school bell rang and getting dressed up to look a couple of years older than we were at twelve, did we really look eighteen?

Furthermore the pornography we may have seen – after a lot of effort and subterfuge – would have been the soft-core variety showing women in various stages of undress, not the extreme hard-core clips that are now practically the only material you see on the web.

Yes, your childhood would have seemed disconcertingly 'adult' to your parents if they compared it to their own. But compared with when you were growing up, your daughter's childhood has been fast-forwarded out of all recognition. The advances in gadgets, phones, broadband – and the changes they have brought – have happened at a dizzying rate in the last decade. In any other era in history, our children – and we as parents – would have had more time to adjust and get used to these developments. Our girls are at risk because a gap has opened up between advances in communication and technology and our knowledge of how they would affect our world. Because we didn't realise how quickly it was happening, we got left behind. It's only now the full effects on girls' development have become obvious that we are starting to catch up.

■■■■ 'We believe in free speech and modern technology.'

Those of us who grew up in and after the sixties like the idea of appearing 'cool' to our children. The image of the fifties-style buttoned-up dad with his pipe and slippers and the mum with a perm and apron still casts a long shadow. The willingness of anyone to speak up has also been hit by the spectre of figures like Mary Whitehouse, who became seen as a national joke for protesting against the 'permissive society'.

No one wants to be cast in the role of the blue-rinsed spoil-sport, scandalised by today's youth – especially as any objections, no matter how sensible, have come to be identified with the right wing and religious fundamentalism. Many mothers I spoke to were also afraid of raising their concerns because they didn't want to appear as joyless, men-hating feminists. They felt other mothers would think they were over-reacting if they complained about sexist attitudes in school, or that they would be unpopular with teachers for being 'troublemakers'.

But by standing back and not getting involved – because we are worried about how we might look if we object – we have let control of the situation slip from our grasp. By not challenging the culture that created these problems, and by allowing the internet to be almost completely unregulated on the grounds of 'free speech', we've let pornography become one of the main preoccupations of the web. In fact, there has been so much free speech, that women are freely allowed to be called 'dumb bitches', 'whores' and 'sluts' on millions of porn sites – yet we feel we have no right of reply against this multi-billion pound global industry.

As parents, the question we now have to ask is who is benefitting from this freedom – and who is really paying the price? The time has come to ask why pornographers, advertisers and strangers have been allowed to say anything to our children, but why we as parents don't feel we can talk back.

██████ 'They'll do it anyway.'

Yes, hard though it may be to come to terms with along the way, eventually our daughters will grow up. But if we raise them well, they will grow at an appropriate pace and find sexual relationships when they are emotionally ready. Hopefully your daughter won't be one of the one in three who lose it on a one-night stand, or the 50 per cent who said it happened when they were drunk. The right time should come because your daughter is in a meaning- ful relationship in which she wants to express her trust and love – and not because her friends are daring her to, or because she feels she needs to keep up with her mates.

If a teenage girl is really determined to have sex, there's realistically not much parents can do to stop it. Somehow and sometime, she will make it happen. But we can set out to ensure that pornography or peer pressure are not behind her decision – and that she is not treated badly because the boy she chooses has grown up using hard-core porn as his sexual template.

THE TWEEN YEARS

The tween years are the years often seen as the lull before the storm in child development. Although this book is written for girls of all ages, it's worth pointing out that, as parents helping our children to defend themselves, this is when we can make the most meaningful impact.

The ages between seven and twelve are a critical period in your daughter's life. Philosopher Rudolf Steiner once described the middle years as the 'root of childhood'; if you look back at your own life, they are probably the years of your childhood you also remember most. During this window, your daughter is just starting to define herself as a separate person away from you. She becomes more curious about the world around her and where she fits in. It's during this time that your daughter will form the foundations of her self-image and self-worth — and it's now that you can help her build herself up.

But because girls are so open at this age, they are also so vulnerable. That's why they need time to think, daydream and work out for themselves where they fit in, free from the stereotypes of what it means to be female, and without being jolted prematurely into prematurely sexual roles. They need time to breathe before the ego-challenging pressures of sex and courtship start to kick in. Ideally, they should be allowed to be themselves.

For now, parents still remain the major influence in a girl's life. It's a period when she will look to you as role models, see your values in practice and take them on board. But before too long, when she moves into the more challenging teen years, part of the process of growing independent is that she will turn away from her family and start listening more to her friends.

Of course it's never too early or too late to start building up your daughter. Every stage of her life is important. It's as critical to protect and nurture a three-year-old as a thirteen-year-old. But by being conscious parents during these building block tween years, your voice will be heard the loudest.

THE ROLE OF MOTHERS

'Every day I hear my mum giving herself a hard time because
she feels overweight, nothing fits her or her face looks wrinkly.
She feels bad about her looks, but I think she is gorgeous.'

ELLA, 13

At the age of eight, Poppy Burge is already following in her mum's footsteps. Mother-of-three Sarah first spotted her daughter's 'flair' for pole-dancing when she was four and started imitating the dance routines of her idol, Miley Cyrus. It's good exercise, Sarah insists, and anyway practising her new hobby does her no more harm than hanging off a climbing frame.

'Poppy is very mature for her age and acts like a mini adult,' explains Sarah. 'She already wears heels, make-up and designer clothes … She takes at least an hour to get ready for her lesson and is never without her lip gloss.'

With heavy blonde extensions and eye make-up, Sarah also takes a lot of care with her appearance. She often disappears from home for a few days to get herself tweaked and improved. Poppy is catching on fast. After all, she is learning it at her mother's knee. When Sarah recently got another top-up of Botox, she asked: 'Mummy, are you making your wrinkles go away?' She has also observed that her mother's breasts have been enhanced by cosmetic surgery, and has since expressed an interest in having hers done when they eventually grow.

So Sarah has already taken the trouble of putting a £7,000 token in her daughter's Christmas stocking to pay for any cosmetic operations her child might want when she is older, calling it an 'investment for the future' and carefully taking inflation into account.

As a mother, Sarah is an extreme example. But she is also a stark illustration of how we can set our girls on a path of endless dissatisfaction with our own quest for never-ending perfection.

Just 2 per cent of adult women feel they are beautiful, according to *The Real Truth about Beauty: A Global Report*. That leaves a huge 98 per cent who feel they are not – and a lot of little girls observing their mums' ongoing unhappiness with the way they look.

Of course many mothers believe letting girls be the prettiest they can be is just child's play. For some parents, giving their daughter a Barbie-doll childhood is an innocent way of rejoicing and celebrating the fact they have a girl. They are reliving their own formative years when they still remember the delight of painting their nails for the first time. But when the demand for the beautification of children becomes so great that our children are already veterans of spa treatments and makeover parties by the time they have left primary school, we need to ask what messages we are sending out about how girls should spend their time and attention.

However sweetly we intend it, by dressing our daughters to look like us, we risk them behaving in ways they aren't emotionally mature enough to handle. Most dangerously, we also let them believe that how they look is the most valuable thing about them.

As our girls' first role models, we need to start setting some boundaries again. I hear many mothers account for the fact their little girls got their ears pierced, or are already in high heels and wearing make-up with the words: 'Once she gets the idea, there's no stopping her.' But it's too early to let children be in charge, and the people who should be stopping them are their parents, by not rubber-stamping the notion in the first place.

We also need to ask some searching questions about where our girls are getting the idea from that they need to be waxed, preened and primed. Is it from the media, from us – or a self-reinforcing combination of both? Anyone who grew up after the sixties grew up in the first media-saturated, appearance-obsessed age. As we became women ourselves, the growing pressure on all women to look better and be slimmer was gradually insinuated into our minds by the proliferation of magazines, TV shows and movies. We have to take great care not to offload our own insecurities onto our daughters – and break the cycle before it gets reinforced again. Otherwise the young girls who innocently observe us fretting all the time about how we look, assume that's just what women do.

As mothers, we need to mentor our children and give them a balanced sense of self-care. Mothers must provide the down-to-earth perspective girls need when they get buffeted by comparisons, competition, faltering confidence and classroom cattiness. We should not be the people teaching them to view life as a catwalk in the first place.

By all means, pass on what you have learned and share your experiences, but resist imposing your ambitions, insecurities and expectations of what she should look like too without searching your own motivations first. Parenting is as much what you don't say as what you do say. There is a difference between being honest and open with your child and blurting out your insecurities for your benefit, not theirs. Sometimes when we are caught off-guard, it can take an almost superhuman act of self-control not to complain that we look dreadful or that we feel like we've gained a few pounds. But your daughter is not your confidante, she is your child. She is not your best friend, she is your ultimate responsibility. So stay conscious of the words you say and the messages you send. Make yours a connection based on all the wonderful things you can share with her – not whether you get your nails and hair highlights done together.

HOW WE TALK TO OUR GIRLS

Even in the most loving, thoughtful families, an amazing amount of gender stereotyping takes place. Some of it is conscious – but much of it is unconscious.

So often, parents diminish their girls by referring to them as 'little dolls', 'poppets' and 'minxes' – or paint them as frail sparrows in need of protection.

We call them princesses – even though the term implies a woman who has done nothing to achieve her status in life except to be the daughter or wife of a high status man.

So often our highest term of praise is 'good girl' – which in fact is often another way of saying that she's compliant, easy to handle and obedient – a sticky label which can eventually stop our girls from expressing their real needs and standing up for themselves.

As parents we need to choose our words carefully. What we say can send off complex and contradictory messages to our girls. Why on the one hand are we encouraging our girls to believe they are as smart and competent as boys, but then undermining them with pet names which imply they are weak and defenceless?

Use language to help your daughter feel strong and independent, not weak and in need of male admiration and protection.

DON'T MAKE CHILDREN
THE BUTT OF YOUR JOKES

Somewhere along the way it became cute and funny to make children into little sexual beings. Turning children into mini-adults is somehow viewed as adorable. Despite the backlash, it is still possible to find romper suits, bibs and toddler T-shirts on the internet with slogans like: 'Sorry, I only date rock-stars', 'All Daddy wanted was a blow job' and worse.

It's almost as if as long as our children don't get it, it's OK for us to have a good laugh at their expense. No doubt, it started with Hollywood films aimed at children, which were meant to keep the parents amused at the same time. Soon scripts became littered with double entendres that were expected to make grown-ups laugh but go over the heads of the younger members of the audience. A few years ago, I attended the afternoon children's show at a family hotel during the Easter half-term with my two girls. Instead of producing a line of bunting from a small boy's T-shirt, in the time-honoured fashion, the entertainer produced several bras tied together. The entertainer had meant to play to the grown-ups in the room, and it raised a small titter. Meanwhile the child looked confused and deeply embarrassed. I wondered why we were laughing at all.

Think about it this way: how can we redraw the boundaries around our children's childhoods if we turn them into comedy? Our children deserve better than to be the butt of our jokes.

THE ROLE OF FATHERS

'My dad was always making remarks about what
women looked like. He rated everyone like a
prize heifer and mainly seemed to value my mum
because she was pretty. As I grew up, I found
myself judging myself on that basis too. It made
me feel I was never pretty enough for any man.'

TESSA, 42

'My husband can't understand why this adoring little girl
has turned into this surly teenager. So he keeps away while
I act as the go-between and sometimes dry the tears.'

TONI, 44

'I was incredibly close to my dad growing up. I just felt so
loved and accepted – and he and my mum made such a
great team. He was the first man who loved me, and he
may be a tough act to follow, but I know I am worth it.'

LAURA, 21

If you are a father reading this, you are the first man in your
daughter's life – and that is a huge responsibility. While she
will look to her mother to learn how to be a woman, she will
look to you for male approval. In a sexualised era where girls are
encouraged by society to please men with the way they look and
act, giving her the security of your unconditional love can be a
very powerful protection.

Of course you may feel that just by going out to work and being the breadwinner and being 'around' as a stable role model, you're doing enough. But your daughter needs you more than that, and a father's semi-present aloofness can be deeply hurtful and confusing to a daughter. To a little girl, being in the same room as a father who is parked behind an iPad or a newspaper can feel like a double betrayal – because you are present, but you still pay her no attention. Because of the way girls tend to blame themselves first, they tend to think it's their fault you don't spend time with them, not because you are busy.

Of course, it's even harder when the perky, eager-to-please daddy's girl turns into a sullen teenager. But at this point it's even more important that fathers don't back off. Resist the temptation to withdraw. Having a father who is involved during the stormy sea of puberty makes a huge difference to how a girl feels about herself at the time. In fact, overall, researchers believe that a father may have even more of a role in building a girl's self-esteem than her mother. While, rightly or wrongly, a girl sees it as her mother's natural role to care for her, she feels like time spent with her dad is his choice.

By giving her the reassurance that you love the person she is becoming, she will face the world more confidently, knowing she can be herself.

The effects of a father's unconditional love are lifelong. According to the Children's Society, daughters of men who were more closely involved in their childhoods develop better friend-ships, more empathy and higher self-worth and are happier with their lives. A father's involvement in a girl's life, as early as toddler-hood, predicts both a girl's self-esteem and her achievements at secondary school. If girls are close to their fathers they are also less likely to have sex at an early age.

On the other hand, researchers have found that girls who are in conflict with their fathers tend to be more aggressive, more bullying and more likely to go off the rails. It may be hard, but just as mothers may have to examine their own attitudes to body image and dieting, as a father you may also have to question your own attitudes to the opposite sex.

Do you value all your daughter's qualities equally? Do you actually listen to her opinion? Or do you minimise and feminise her when there is no real need? When it comes to your partner, do you treat her mother as an equal? Or have you started to lump her and your daughter together as a mysterious, alien species of womanhood you will never understand? If you do pay your daughter compliments, do you find yourself constantly congratulating her for being a compliant 'good girl', compared to your son? Crucially, do you ever judge your daughter by what she looks like? Do you affectionately or approvingly refer to her as a heartbreaker or a 'little cracker', or joke that you'll need to fight the boys off when she's older? If so, be aware of how your daughter could turn those messages back on herself. A University of Auckland survey of more than 200 daughters of men who put high importance on a woman's appearance found that they were much more likely to have made themselves sick to lose weight. Every single one of these girls believed they were fatter than they should be.

More dangerously, if you turn away from your daughter, girls start to wonder how they need to change – or what they need to do differently – to get you to notice them. As parenting educators Ian and Mary Grant observe in their book *Raising Confident Girls*, some of the most rebellious teenage girls became that way when their fathers took a hands-off approach in their adolescent years. 'It's as if the girls had something inside them that made them test their fathers to see if they would fight for them.'

When helping your daughter grow up, don't feel disadvantaged just because you're not female yourself. The fact that you are less likely to be caught up in the sometimes fractious relationships between mothers and daughters means you can help keep the ship steady. Your point of view is also invaluable because you can 'decode' how males think for her. Don't fall into the trap of telling her: 'They're only after one thing.' Assure her there will be good men out there who will value her – and she should reserve the right to choose those men carefully.

Above all, make your love unconditional. Because men tend to be more target-driven, don't think it's your role to set goals for your daughter. When your five-year-old daughter learns to swim a width, resist the temptation to immediately urge her to try a length. To a girl, elated by her new achievement, it sounds like a criticism that she hasn't done enough. Celebrate her efforts, not just the end result. Love her for who she is, not just for how good she looks – or makes you look.

Without being overly protective, let her know you are always there for her. By treating her with dignity and respect, set the standard that she will expect other men to follow. By giving your acceptance, you can save her needing to prove her worth to men – because she knows how valuable and lovely she is to you.

WHAT YOU CAN DO

🎔 **Start early**. Fathers often feel excluded by the mother-daughter relationship. When a baby cries for its mother first, some men feel rejected – and quickly retreat into the belief that a girl only needs her mum. From an early age, get involved and stay involved.

❊ **Don't make it 'women's work'.** The battle to protect our daughters' self-worth is not just a mother's job. It is not something that should just be left to a community of like-minded mothers and feminist campaigners. Remember your part in helping our girls grow into women who seek out healthy relationships.

❊ **Work around your daughter.** In these days when more of us are able to work from home with more flexible hours, look at ways you could be more involved in your girl's day-to-day life. If you work full-time out of the home, find out how to prioritise time with her. She won't be a child for long.

❊ **Find things you can do together.** Set aside – and stick to – a regular, uninterrupted special time for you and your daughter to spend together. Let her decide what you do together so she feels she has some control in your relationship. Don't lecture. Just be together.

❊ **Don't judge other women's looks in front of your daughter.** Never denigrate any female – or put her on a pedestal – purely on the basis of looks alone (and especially not weight), as your daughter will think all men will judge *her* on that basis.

❊ **Keep hugging.** Fathers may feel less comfortable about cuddling their girls as they get older. But keep showing your affection physically, even if it's just a squeeze or a stroke of the hand.

❊ **Be fair.** If you also have sons, invite both girls and boys to do the same activities to teach your daughters they have equal abilities.

❄ **Don't make her into your little girl in need of protection.**
It makes dads feel fatherly and macho to see their daughters as delicate flowers. But feeling competent is a major pillar of self-worth, so don't take it away from her by making her feel incapable. Encourage her to feel she can do anything boys can do by teaching her traditionally male skills, like DIY or car mechanics.

❄ **Ask her mum to be a go-between.** If you're unsure what's happening with your daughter, ask her mother for some translation, rather than asking your daughter outright or blundering into it. She may well be sensitive about her growing body in ways you may not be aware of.

❄ **Never tease her about her appearance.** She may laugh along, but girls are so sensitive that even the most gentle mickey-taking and nicknames are never forgotten – or forgiven.

BUILDING AN EXTENDED FAMILY

As much as we try to be everything to our children, it helps to have other people around who also have their best interests at heart. When your views carry less sway with her in her teen years, the presence of other responsible adults who share your values – and who your daughter respects – can have a steadying effect, especially when your input isn't always appreciated.

Our growing sense of isolation from family and our bigger community is one of the reasons anxiety levels have risen in society. Counteract this trend by nurturing relationships with aunts, grandparents and family friends who will be there for her if she wants to talk about subjects she can't address with you.

Introduce her to strong, independent women in your family who she can respect and model herself on. It can be a big boost to a child's self-esteem to know that there are other grown-ups who want to spend time with her even though they don't have to. Quite simply the world feels like a safer place.

Although it is harder after the primary school years, make an active effort to get to know the mothers of your daughter's friends. Invite other parents in for a cup of tea when they drop off their children. Attend PTA social events to get a feel for the values of the parents of the children your daughter spends time with.

As she gets older, it will help to know that there are other adults looking out for her, who hopefully have similar priorities – and you will be in a better position to understand the school landscape your daughter is living in.

THE ROLE OF SCHOOLS

While it's true that parents bear the first responsibility, it's a far bigger challenge than can be handled by families alone. Schools can play a vital role in helping parents decide and uphold the values that will make their children stronger. Not only can they help hold the line, they can also assist parents as a group to be more mindful about how to protect children's well-being.

But while some schools are progressive, there are still plenty who are sleep-walking and turning a blind eye to sexist messages which should not be part of school life. Where once there were face-painting stalls at primary school fairs, increasingly there are makeover tents where children can get manicures and hair extensions, thereby endorsing the idea that the most important thing females have to think about is how they look. At the very places where girls should be learning that their minds matter, they are being told it's never too young to start taking part in time-consuming adult beauty rituals.

There are plenty of other examples of lapses of judgement. At one Kent primary school, the head teacher defended a decision to invite a pole-dancing academy to perform at the school fête on the grounds that the troupe was demonstrating a fun way to keep fit. But while gymnastics does involve swinging off poles and suppleness, once it's done in crop tops and full make-up, it's disingenuous to pretend that pole-dancing does not come with sexualised overtones.

Some head teachers may argue that it's the Parents' Association that organises such events, and that there's nothing they can do.

But it remains the person at the top of the school who bears the responsibility for setting a more enlightened tone, by letting their own views be known and steering the curriculum towards sending positive messages to children.

In the smaller arena of the classroom, teachers also need to tread carefully in their direct interaction. One fourteen-year-old told me her teacher had organised a joke end-of-year 'alternative' prize-giving. She had been voted 'girl most likely to wear the most make-up' by her classmates. To be a good sport, she pretended to take it with good grace – even though the reason she wore foundation was to cover her spots. Privately, she was devastated.

As a parent you have a voice – and PTAs are generally dying for volunteers, so you always have the chance to be heard. As Diane Levin suggests in her book *So Sexy So Soon*, the best way for schools and parents to work together is by creating an atmosphere where teachers and parents co-operate, share information and help each other with how to limit children's exposure to the harmful effects of early sexualisation. 'When this happens,' she says, 'it's a win-win situation for everyone but the marketers.'

WHAT YOU CAN DO

- **Ask schools to be mindful of the messages they send out.** There are plenty of inappropriate messages being passed around via joke award ceremonies, satirical magazines and suggestive musical numbers in dance clubs and school discos. Without wishing to sound too PC, some schools could be more thoughtful. Don't apologise or go silent if something slips through the net. You don't have to be strident or difficult or embarrass your child. But in order to protect your daughter, you need a voice too. Other parents or the head teacher don't have to agree with the points you raise, but at least your objections will get them thinking about it.

- **Make building self-worth a priority for your child's teacher.** If you feel your child has low self-esteem then talk to her teachers so they are aware of your worries. Quiet, under-confident children are often allowed to fade into the background. Then, when your daughter is never picked, it confirms her poor opinion of herself. Ask teachers to help you find ways of breaking this cycle, and choose a school for your child which makes building self-worth a top priority. Teachers who have favourites in the class, who are predisposed towards the alpha group or who don't make efforts to include more reticent children should be called out. It's lazy teaching.

A word on proms

'Anya is a little madam and my only child, so she gets what she wants. All I do is keep her happy. Yes, there is parent pressure at prom time. You can't be the parent who sends his daughter to the prom in rags. Do all the girls compare themselves to each other? Yes, but that's women. I can't change that. Like every dad, I think my daughter is beautiful, so I'm not going to set a budget on her dress or her limo. This is about making memories.'

BARRY, FATHER OF ANYA, ELEVEN

'It's exciting because it's an opportunity to shine and look pretty. All the spotlight is on you. In the back of

the limo, I will be with my friends, having girly chats
about the boys in our class and our lifestyle.'

TONIA, ELEVEN

When Rachel watched her eleven-year-old daughter Megan being
swept off in a sports car to her school prom last summer, it was an
emotional moment. After all, Megan was wearing a £200 glittery
fuchsia ball gown. Her face was expertly made up with lip gloss,
foundation and mascara, and her long brown locks were artfully
styled into a cascade of curls. Megan had simply never looked so
grown-up – or attracted more compliments for doing so.

As a single mother, it was a stretch for Rachel to find the
money it cost to make sure Megan looked the part. In this
unwelcome game of playground one-upmanship, it seemed that
nothing was ever quite enough.

'The prom meant everything to Megan,' Rachel told me. 'She
started planning what dress she wanted to wear a year before,
and talked about nothing else in the run-up to the end of term.
Most of the stress was to do with the girls comparing each other
and worrying about who would look the prettiest. Then Megan
kept coming home to me and saying: "So-and-so says her dress
is costing thousands" or "So-and-so is having hair extensions and
fake nails." You don't know whether it's true or not – but they
were all talking about it all the time.'

Apart from the vast amount of mental space it took up in
her daughter's mind, there was also Rachel's concern that the
prom encouraged Megan to act and behave in ways she was not
yet ready for.

'She is quite tomboyish and sporty so this was the first time
she has had her make-up done. She knows she doesn't need to
wear it, but she worried that if she didn't wear it at the prom,

she wouldn't fit in. They all have to have a boy to go with too. Megan's already got a playground boyfriend, and she kept asking him what he thought she should wear.'

Before the advent of US-style proms around five years ago, the end of primary school would have been marked with the signing of autograph books and maybe a school disco. But while no one wants to be the killjoy, it may also be worthwhile for parents to question the advisability of the increasingly lavish Hello!-style end-of-term events that have replaced these more low-key send-offs.

Once a big deal to look forward to when they left school at eighteen, giving children proms at the age of ten and eleven means adult behaviours are foisted on them before they are ready. Many end up feeling they have to act out roles they are not entirely comfortable with. If left unchecked, such events can become a lightning rod for cliquishness and exclusion, and can encourage children to mimic and judge themselves by adult A-list standards of beauty before it has naturally occurred to them to do so.

As one mother told me, the event made it clear who was 'in' and who was 'out' with brutal clarity: 'My daughter Ruby came home devastated after she'd been told at school there was no space in the limousine with the popular girls, when apparently there was. It was a scramble to find who else she could go with.'

In every school, there are always parents who welcome such proms with open arms – often as an opportunity to showboat their children's social status and position in the class beauty stakes. But all too often, it leaves the remaining parents feeling like they have no choice but to help their children keep up at any cost.

As one teacher told me: 'The child also comes home and tells the parents so-and-so has got a special dress that's worth this much, and she's getting her hair and nails done too. Pretty soon, the parents feel unable to say no for fear of their child being the odd one out. In the process, it's easy for mums and dads to lose sight of what's good for children. The competition drives them to a point past which they might not normally go.'

Indeed, in order to give them their sought-after 'red carpet moment', parents are paying for their primary school age girls to have fake tans and hair removal. Teachers have come across mothers buying breast enhancers – known as 'chicken fillets' – to fill in for their girls' non-existent cleavage. In other cases, the girls themselves simply used the time-honoured technique of stuffing toilet paper down their tops. Many boys feel similarly under pressure to 'choose a date' when they don't yet have any interest in forming proto-romantic relationships.

Educational consultant Chris Calland, who goes into schools to talk to children about body image, says: 'This is all putting a lot of emphasis on image and looks at a very vulnerable point in their development where they really are just gaining their identity. It's artificial. If you are a girl getting the false nails, the make-up and the tan for a school event, you are being told at eleven that it's OK to pretend to be something that you are not.' After all, this is her chance for a girl to show how well she is living up to the expectations that today's society has for her about how she is supposed to look and behave, how much she is admired by boys and how popular she is.

These days every moment of the lead-up to prom – the hairstyles, the manicures, the trying-on of the dress, the limo ride – is relentlessly captured on Facebook and other social networks, encouraging girls to value their images first and foremost. By working so hard to attract as many likes as possible for their dresses and hairstyles, it also provides girls with an early lesson on how to be shaped by other people's approval, and how important it is to compete – and win – against other girls.

The end result is that proms become a status update for how a young girl is doing on her journey to becoming a woman. They are damaging because they come at an age when she is not yet in a position to analyse or reject the messages these events give her.

WHAT YOU CAN DO

✂ **Question the need for Hollywood-style proms before children are ready.** If schools want to encourage primary school boys and girls to mix better, ask them to think about more neutral activities – like outward-bound days – that don't make children feel they should be thinking about each other romantically. If the school insists on putting on discos, let children know they don't have to go in boy-girl couples, and stress that it's fine to go in groups of friends. Russell Hobby, general secretary of the National Association of Head Teachers, believes 'low-key' celebrations – which involve parents – are a better idea for children this age. He said: 'These events should be appropriate for that stage of life, rather than bringing forward the kind of adult-style event the sixteen- and eighteen-year-olds are having. There may be one or two disgruntled parents if a head says no to a prom. But most parents are very reasonable and would appreciate a steer. It's part of the head's job to set the tone and atmosphere of the school.'

PART TWO

How Building Self-Worth and Communication Is Your Daughter's Best Defence

SELF-WORTH

Take a browse through the social media pages of tweens and teenagers and they look confident, brazen even. They pout, pull faces and show off for the camera. After all, by the age of thirteen they are already masters of their own universe as they project their own idealised avatars into cyberspace.

But scratch the surface and you may find it's not real confidence, but something more brittle: bravado borrowed from pop videos and celebrity gossip culture. It's the belief that being able to project a narrow concept of beauty gives you 'confidence'.

In fact, statistics on depression, anxiety and self-harm show our girls are more brittle than their sassy exteriors suggest. Their sense of self is based too much on where they come in the classroom beauty pageant, how 'hot' boys think they are and how they score in the popularity stakes.

From every direction, our girls are being inundated with messages that they have to be thinner, prettier, cleverer, sexier, richer and better dressed. Advertisers, the internet, the magazine and fashion industries and television get children hooked by telling them they are simply not good enough, hot enough or cool enough.

Of course as parents, our ultimate goal should be a society where those messages are moderated. But until that happens, we need to inoculate our daughters by helping them develop a strong sense of self-acceptance.

Actively thinking about how to help your daughter develop a secure core will help to immunise her against any need she may feel in her teenage years to win approval from her peers through behaviour that's harmful to her – or from the insecurities that will lead her to feel she has to conform to the 'so sexy' stereotype.

By building up her inner self, the only wounds from the negative messages around her will hopefully be small nicks which will heal over without causing too much long-term damage. They won't shake her inner self because ultimately she will know herself better than that. Overall, she will feel she is likeable and not stick in panic to cliques who may encourage her to act against her true self. Ultimately, she will tend to feel in control and make better choices because she knows, likes and trusts herself. She will be happier being an individual who makes her own judgements and decisions.

There are a lot of parenting books out there on subjects ranging from how be a fabulous mum to how to make your child into a genius. There are entire shelves devoted to the skills you need to get children into routines, deal with toddler tantrums and handle potty training. But beyond that, there is not so much available on the single most important way to ensure the happiness and emotional safety of your child – or how to prove to her that she is already good enough.

Of course, all parents set out with the vague and general aim of wanting their daughters to feel good about themselves. But it's a question of how much priority we give this goal, amid our need to see our children get good exam results, be 'successful' and reflect well on us. I hear a lot of parents rush to say how 'bright' their children are, patting themselves on the back about when they get a string of A* GCSEs, A-levels and university offers. But I rarely hear them extol qualities which are ultimately more important, like having a healthy sense of who they are. Because with all the good looks, popularity and exam success in the world, our girls will never be truly happy or successful without that.

That's why developing a healthy inner life should be the first and ultimate goal, not a by-product that we hope she picks up along the way. Self-worth is not 'big-headedness', or the sort of cocky, self-conscious, superficial confidence we see in so many young people. It's not 24-hour-a-day full-on look-at-me fabulousness that comes from conformity to today's narrow definition of beauty. Inflated self-regard, based on empty praise, narcissism, self-centredness and the need to show off, is nothing like a solid sense of self-appreciation, based in reality. Self-acceptance is simply about feeling good about yourself most of the time. It's the ability to understand your feelings, and using that understanding to know what makes you feel good and what makes you feel bad.

Here are just some of the benefits your daughter will reap from a healthy sense of self-worth. The good news is that, at the same time, every single one will double up and protect her from the effects of undermining messages.

* She won't desperately need the approval of her peer group over everything she does or wears.

* She will know herself well enough to be able to brush off and fight off bitchy put-downs. If she's bullied, she will know it's not her fault.

* She won't seek out unhappy sex to make her feel wanted, desirable or worthwhile.

* She won't believe she is defined by what she owns or wears.

* She will choose partners who are worthy of her and will choose healthy relationships over unhealthy ones.

* She will take good risks because she has the belief and trust in herself to find out what she is truly capable of.

* She will forgive herself for failure and will get back up again.

How to create a growth mindset

Children can start feeling trapped and hopeless when they feel they have no control to change themselves or the world around them. Because they don't have the benefit of perspective or the autonomy of adults, how it is now is how they think it will always be.

In teenagers, this can develop into feelings of low mood or, at worst, depression.

One of the greatest gifts you can give your daughter is the belief that she always has the power to grow and change. In other words, she has free will. Instead of letting her believe that traits like intelligence or temperament are fixed from birth, explain that she can get better at anything. Praise qualities of character she has control over, like persistence and effort, to create a more can-do attitude. On a smaller scale, it means your daughter will be able to look forward to a better day if the one she is having is not so great. On a bigger scale, it will send her the message she can always evolve and make whatever situation she is in better.

Fostering self-esteem through competence

Have you ever seen the huge and natural smile your child has when she has done something all by herself for the first time? Every time your child feels that sensation, it's another building block in her self-esteem. Self-worth does not just come from us telling our children they are capable and clever, although acknowl-edgement can help when it's sincere and targeted. Children also need to feel self-worth from within themselves too.

But it's ironic that the faster our girls grow up in the cyber-world, the less we allow them to prove what they are capable of in the real world. In a climate of fear abetted by round-the-clock television news and alarm over paedophiles, it's very tempting to go the other way and overprotect our daughters in everything they do. While we may think we are safeguarding them from injury and physical harm, really we are also denying our children the chance to feel good, explore nature, climb trees and learn to look after themselves.

The result is that one in ten parents don't let their children play outside because it's dirty, according to a survey by the Children's Society, and one in five seven- to fourteen-year-olds play outside for less than an hour a week. Yet nearly two in five children complain they don't play outdoors as much as they would like. By condemning our girls to a battery hen existence and allowing them to be glued to computers, just so we know where we can find them, they enter a world of cyber dangers where the threats are different, but in their own ways just as great.

Denying children independence and responsibility is taken by them to mean we have no confidence in their abilities. While you may hope cosseting them makes them feel safe and cared for, in fact they feel helpless. Because childhood is a process of learning to do new things, children believe you are waiting on them hand and foot because they are incapable. Ultimately, it also undermines your authority – and you will need every ounce of that in the years to come. As parenting educator Noel Janis-Norton points out: 'Children don't respect servants.'

So, check that your fears about your daughter's safety and well-being are in proportion to reality. Ask yourself who you are really protecting here. Is it her? Or are you doing it for your own peace of mind? Whether it's making an omelette or changing a light bulb, think first about what your daughter is ready to do for herself – not what you can do for her.

CONNECTION AND CREATING A SANCTUARY

Why we must stay present and find more time

Once again, let's go back to the beginning. From the moment we first held our baby girls in our arms, we promised we would try to be the best possible parents. We vowed to read the right child-rearing books, say the right things and spend all the time we had playing and caring for these delightful little creatures.

Indeed, the first part of building our daughters' self-worth should have been blissfully easy. When they cried and we responded by picking them up, we taught them the first lesson in feeling good about themselves – that they are valued people who deserve to be heard. As our babies grew into toddlers, we continued to work hard to help our girls grow up well by cuddling and playing with them.

But somewhere along the way other pressures, like work and the need to earn money, started to steal away the hours we meant to spend with our little girls. Gradually, day by day, then year by year, many of us became less and less the mothers and fathers we set out to be.

Over time, did the time you once devoted to sitting down and playing puzzles with your daughter dwindle – and did you start to see the fact that your child was settled and playing quietly as an opportunity to grab ten minutes to catch up on email?

If this sounds like you, you are not alone. Modern technology and economic uncertainty have joined forces to make our working days longer, and more parents than ever are both working. A total of 66 per cent of mothers now have jobs, compared with 23 per cent in 1971, and often with little family support to help them juggle both roles.

All this hurrying means that study after study finds working parents have a shrinking amount of time with their children. After a long working day, half of parents now say they are too stressed and tired to read their kids a bedtime story, even though that simple act is one of the easiest ways to make a child feel valued.

Furthermore, the more stressed we get, the less empathetic and more impatient our parenting becomes. We are so busy keeping ourselves afloat that all we want is our children to do what we say without question. Our standards slip – we become patchy about sticking to them and we default to 'anything for a quiet life', where it's easy for us to let our children be entertained by technology so that we get a break.

The saddest thing is that the children from stressed families often process all this by feeling they are to blame. Our unhappiness leads them to believe we don't like them very much.

According to child psychologist and author David Elkind: 'Young children – two to eight years – tend to perceive hurrying as a rejection, as evidence that their parents do not really care about them.' He points out that these feelings of rejection follow our children into their teens, 'the time when they pay us back for all the sins, real or imagined, that we committed against them when they were children'.

So don't make the mistake of thinking your children don't notice when your eyes flick down to your latest text, just because it's become normal or because they've given up complaining. If we only half-listen and allow all our time to become enveloped by the creeping tendrils of technology, we risk losing our essential bond.

The fact is that you can tell your daughter you love her a dozen times a day, but if you are texting and looking up at the clock as you do it, the message will be undermined. And what would you do if someone was usually looking the other way when you talked to them? You'd give up.

It sounds corny, but children really do spell the word 'love' as 'time'. Sometimes we just need reminding that it's running out. Our girls' childhoods are short. From birth to the age of twelve, we have just 4,380 days with them. Yet sometimes we are so busy trying to give our girls everything materially, we don't give them what they need most – us.

It's a corrosive atmosphere that can create separations that can be hard to heal. If we spend their formative years glued to laptops and tablets, is it any surprise our daughters stop looking up from their screens when we enter the room by the time they are teenagers? It's a catch 22 on so many levels. The less time you spend with your children, the less interesting you will find them – and the more your eyes will switch back to the latest incoming message.

Many parents try to get by with an ongoing promise that things will get better soon. But, as family educator Rob Parsons of Care for the Family points out: 'A slower day is not coming.' Still, while it's true that you won't ever have more time, what you can do is prioritise what you do have. You can pay less attention to the things that don't really matter – like celebrity culture and television – and spend more time on the things that really do – like your children.

The good news is that it is never too late to adjust the emotional temperature in your home – and the effects will be instantaneous. Putting boundaries around your work, placing limits on your technology use and taking steps to de-stress – all of these things will have an immediate effect.

Holding ordinary conversations, playing games, doing simple things together – like cooking and going for walks – are all you need to do. But it's time that needs to be set aside and protected.

Making your home into a sanctuary

Remember that you set the emotional thermostat of your home. You control how many influences enter from the outside and how secure and safe it feels for your children. If the world feels like a stressful and critical place where they are finding it difficult to cope, it's easy for children to turn to media to regain power and control of their lives. So, more than ever, your home needs to be a place where your girl can relax and recharge her batteries – and where you can spend time together.

Teach your daughter how to spot the signs that she is feeling tense and reactive and needs to de-stress. Ask her to imagine a sliding scale, marked out with the numbers one to ten. When she feels she's getting overloaded, suggest she has a warm bath, curls up with you on the sofa with a cup of hot chocolate, asks you for a back rub or takes some exercise. All of these are small things, but together they give her the message that she always has a sanctuary she can go where she can feel safe.

As Dr Joan Borysenko, a Harvard-trained expert on stress, says, simple awareness can be the best protection. One method she suggests works well for children and parents alike. 'Create a sliding scale in your head. At one end, the number one means: "I'm feeling really good" and ten is "I'm feeling burnt out". Keep drawing a hatched line between those two points to work out where you stand. If it gets to an eight, and you're feeling like you can't stand it anymore, it's time to take a moment to relieve the situation.'

WHAT YOU CAN DO

❄ **Take family holidays.** The breaks we take as families are so often what people remember about their childhoods. By stepping out from the daily pressures of your everyday lives for a few days – and getting a break from technology – you can keep the bond between you and your child strong, and put the fun back into your relationship.

❄ **Give her a healthy diet.** Make girls stronger by giving them balanced meals, free from additives and sugar. It's said so often that it has become a cliché, but sending children off with a good breakfast of slow-release carbohydrates and protein really does set them up for the day.

❄ **Get a pet.** If they can fit into your family life, pets are a wonderful way to make a home cosier. They also get children out of the house, release feel-good endorphins and offer an innocent distraction from the pressures of the outside world. Giving them responsibility for the welfare of another living being also helps children learn why boundaries and routine are important.

Help her get a good night's sleep
Technology, homework and the expansion of after-school activities are all conspiring to mean that most children are sleep-deprived. Researchers have found children get over an hour less sleep every night than they did a decade ago. But although their

lives may have become increasingly busy, youngsters' needs have not changed. They need around eleven hours of sleep at the age of five, ten and a half hours at eight, ten hours at age nine, nine and a half hours at eleven and nine hours at age fourteen, according to NHS recommendations.

While parents do their best to stick to bedtime routines for the first few years, very often they back off when their children reach secondary school. But, if anything, you need to be more watchful when your daughter hits the teenage years, due to the increasing demands of school work and round-the-clock technology. Lack of sleep in teens has been linked to depression, self-harm and poor exam results. Those who have not slept enough are more prone to negative emotions such as fear, anger and poor behaviour, leading to rows and disconnection.

So, help your daughter to spot the signs that she is getting exhausted and overwrought. At a neutral time, not when she is already beside herself with fatigue, explain how sleep will boost both her mood and concentration.

The importance of play

If you look back to your favourite snapshot memories from your own childhood, there's a good chance you will remember moments of self-discovery you had when you were playing outside somewhere on your own. Maybe it was seeing how high you could go on a swing or making a den in the back garden with no adults anywhere around, so any achievement was all yours.

Once, children had two educations – the one they had at school and the one they had from nature. It is in these moments, when kids are truly carefree, away from grown-up intervention, that they first start to learn who they are and what they are capable of.

When UNICEF researchers asked children their requirements for happiness they named not only time with families and friends, but also time spent outdoors. Yet at the same time, as the pressures on our daughters are growing, we have unwittingly taken away the very experiences that allow them to grow and become self-reliant in the first place.

Past generations of children have endured worse kinds of stress, like war and famine and separation from parents. While the dangers today are not as extreme, they are much more persistent.

While children have been spending less time outside, childhood mental disorders have been increasing.

While it's recognised that boys need to get out of the house to burn off some energy, this need is less recognised in girls. But girls also need everyday adventures to work out who they are and what they can do, time to learn how their bodies work and to explore the world. So try backing off. Allow them to get bored and go outside. Instead of drawing up a timetable for them worthy of a CEO, let them stay at home more and just be quietly available.

When they spend time alone, make sure it is in nature, not just with an iPad. Limit what educationalist Sue Palmer calls 'junk play'. Apply the 80/20 rule. Sue says: 'If a girl has 80 per cent real play during childhood, she should gradually learn to make her own choices about the best way to negotiate the junk play jungle.'

VALUES AND BOUNDARIES

Deciding on values

Considering how much time we spend worrying about feeding, clothing and schooling our children, it's ironic how little time we spend thinking about the central messages we want to pass on to them. Despite having been teens ourselves, so often we are not sure where we stand when our girls reach the same stage in life. While we may fret about E-numbers and school league tables, how much thought do we give to the values we want our girls to live by?

One of the reasons parents have been left drowning in the sea of today's challenges is that we may have never sat down and taken the time to decide what those values are. In our more live-and-let-live society, it has been left to us to decide on our priorities. But most often, we've ended up not deciding on anything much at all. Is it OK for your daughter to go on Facebook before the legal age of thirteen because some of her mates are on it? Should she be allowed to wear make-up to school? Instead of thinking about these things, we put off these difficult questions and fire-fight when rows flare up. But by time the dilemma has surfaced, the whole situation is fraught and often whipped into a frenzy by peer pressure.

Whatever you decide, you will be in a much better position if, as parents, you have given some thought first to where you stand. If you do, there's a better chance that you will be able to send out a steady stream of consistent messages on which you and your partner can base your joint decisions.

But even once you've decided on your values, all of this could do more harm than good if you don't stick to them. When our words contradict our actions, our children take the most note of what we do, not what we say. It's not just enough to spell it out, you have to live by your values too. If words and actions conflict, children lose respect for both.

Your values and others

Once you have decided upon some of your values, be confident enough to be clear about them to friends, family, teachers and other parents. Uphold your right to ask others to support the way you want to bring up your daughter – especially if you feel they are encouraging her to grow up faster than you would wish.

When it comes to holding the line about what is good for your daughter, it may be that other parents around you have not had the chance to think about the issues. Sometimes explaining your own reasons for wanting to protect your daughter may help them consider the implications if they have not thought about them already.

For example, if you've worked hard to avoid your eight-year-old thinking she needs make-up to look pretty and she's invited to a party where make-up is encouraged, say: 'Thanks – but not for my child.' After all, why, after your careful consideration, would you let another parent undermine your concern for what's healthiest for your child and start planting the idea that she needs make-up in your child's mind before she is ready? Pandora's box only needs to be opened once.

As your daughter grows, dilemmas like this will be unavoidable. But coming from a family where there are clear boundaries will help her make better decisions for herself.

I know it's hard. My younger daughter has friends with

underage Instagram accounts, and so she wanted one too. But if you explain early on that different families have different values and priorities – and why, as I did in this case, you would prefer your daughter to see the world first-hand rather than as a series of images to upload to her profile – children will accept your reasons, and you will have safeguarded a little more of their childhood.

The same goes for giving them reasons about not being able to try alcohol before the legal age. In our home, I will be saying no on the grounds that it's an intoxicant that is dangerous for a girl's developing body and makes her vulnerable. Of course, I won't be there when my daughters are offered tumblers of vodka and litre bottles of cider at parties. But if they know and understand our reasons, which have been in place for as long as they remember, and understand there are good reasons for them, they will be better able to find their own moral compasses.

WHAT YOU CAN DO

❊ **Get on the same page as your partner – and keep talking.** If you are seriously both at odds over parenting values, your daughter will dismiss you both, and consider that neither of you knows what you are talking about. Find a middle way you can both agree on for the sake of your daughter.

❊ **Let her defer to your values if she's not ready to hold the line herself.** Even though your girl will be developing her own values, they can still be hard to uphold in the face of peer group pressure. So allow her to use you as her excuse. If her friend wants to know why she can't text back at midnight, let her blame you because you long ago made it a strict house rule never to allow phones in bedrooms after 9pm. Give her a code word to use so she can call you from anywhere and secretly let you know that she is in a situation she is not comfortable with, so you can come and get her.

Creating boundaries

It may sound contradictory, but giving children rules is what allows them the freedom to become independent, strong people.

Consistency is the best way for your daughter to feel accepted for who she is. She will be safer being herself, without having to follow the herd. To a girl trying to find her way, the world actually feels a more secure place when strong, consistent boundaries are drawn for her. Further down the line, she is less likely to feel the need to assert her individuality through unhappy sex – or fall victim to negative peer pressure.

But, as helpful as it is to decide on your boundaries, make sure you and your partner impart them consistently, because the words 'because I say so' simply won't wash. It's also not enough to make generalised pronouncements like 'be yourself' or 'always tell the truth'. You need to show how these concepts play out in the real world.

Every girl will face difficult situations. So, help her role play how to react when she will be called upon to use her values under pressure – like what she would do if she were sent an embarrassing picture of a classmate. Strong values will give her the backbone to resist what is not good for her. Imagine the common scenarios. Look at news stories about young people and talk together about the dilemmas facing young girls today and what she thinks.

Children may look like they don't care, but deep down they

want to know that they are being raised by honourable and honest grown-ups. Experienced mothers have told me that after the turbulent years passed, their daughters thanked them for holding the line. After all, it's the girls who've just come through it who know better than anyone the pressures out there.

WHAT YOU CAN DO

- **Tell her why the rules are in place.** Show your daughter that boundaries are not there just because you have the power to impose them, but to keep her safe.

- **Give her some input.** Of course, as parents, we ultimately draw up the rules. But rather than arbitrarily imposing them, ask your daughter some questions about what she thinks they should be. If your values have rubbed off on her, you may be pleasantly surprised by the common sense answers. By thinking hard about them, rather than having them foisted on her, they will make more sense to her.

- **Ask her to think about what is age appropriate.** Ask her why she thinks legal ages are in place. Discuss with her the legal age for drinking, smoking and sex so she sees that they apply to the whole of society, not just to her.

EMOTIONAL INTELLIGENCE

At a time when the pressure on girls is unprecedented, one of the greatest skills you can teach your daughter is how to regulate her emotions. Although girls are often seen as having a wider range of complex feelings at an earlier age than boys, that does not mean they know how to control them.

Helping girls to develop emotional intelligence is as important to their success in life as teaching them reading, writing or arithmetic. If you give your child the gift of insight, she will learn to recognise how she really feels and why. Help her to know herself by never dismissing her problems or trying to solve them for her. The more you give your girl the skills to understand herself and solve her own dilemmas, the more in control she will feel in a confusing world. When faced with risky situations, like manipulative boyfriends or undermining friends, emotional intelligence will ultimately help her recognise what is damaging to her – and what is not.

WHAT YOU CAN DO

- **Show her how to name – and respond to – the negative voices in her head.** When a girl hears a voice which is telling her she's not good enough, she tends to assume it is right. Tell her that just because she hears it, it doesn't mean she has to listen.

- **Tell her sadness is nothing to be ashamed of.** Teach your daughter to recognise what sadness is and to give it time to pass. If she believes these feelings are uncomfortable or anxiety-making for you, she will start to conceal them – and begin to disconnect from you. That emotion could then resurface later in a potentially more toxic form. Assure her that she will always survive heartache and eventually another feeling will take its place.

⚜ Show her how to replace negative thoughts with positive ones. For example, if that inner voice tells her, 'You can't do this', show her she can substitute that thought with: 'This might be tricky, but I can learn.' Help her give a name to her self-critical voices – like the Gremlin or Ms Mean – so she can recognise that they are something outside herself which she can choose to ignore.

⚜ Let her solve her own problems. Teach responsibility. Don't allow her to blame you for the fact she hasn't done her homework or can't find anything suitable in her wardrobe to wear because everything's still dirty in her un-emptied overnight bag. By all means, listen patiently to what she has to say when she's upset or angry, and summarise it back to her so she knows you have understood. Ask her to question herself about the reasons, rather than get angry, so she can work out what to do next time.

⚜ Ask her why she thinks people act the way they do. People's behaviour and motivations – which are so often contradictory and hard to fathom even for adults – can be confusing and scary for girls. Trying to ascribe motivations is always a hit-and-miss game. But if another child has said something to upset her, try helping her to see the context behind it. If you can help her see the remarks in perspective, you can help make her aware of the complexities of human behaviour, and help her realise that she is not to blame if someone is cruel to her. Tell her she can't control other people. She can only control how she responds to them.

❖ **Explain your own emotions and reasons.** Give your life some subtitles so she can understand why you do the things you do and can learn from them. Don't just say: 'because I say so' or 'that's just the way it is'. Let her know why you might be feeling angry or sad, so she realises it's not about something she's done. Girls are so sensitive they will often automatically assume they are to blame.

❖ **Give your daughter a 'big picture' way of looking at life.** Ask her to look for an answer to the questions: 'Why am I here?' and 'What can I do to make the world a better place by being in it?' She doesn't have to answer. By giving her a hint of something beyond herself, she's less likely to put long-lasting importance on trivial things like consumerism and looks.

❖ **Respect your child's opinion.** Don't dismiss your daughter's views because she's a child. Contrary to the image of the compliant 'good girl', the fact that a child is developing a strong sense of self may mean she starts arguing her point of view. From the age of seven, children pride themselves on being logical and fair, so don't shout down their arguments, tiring though it may be to listen.

❖ **Treat your daughter as though she is already the best person she can be.** This isn't the same as forcing children to fit your expectations. It's about appealing to the best in their nature to be an honest, decent person. Never stereotype a child as difficult. See it as a sign she is reacting to the fear she is losing her connection with you. Take steps to get close again.

🗶 **Ask your child to be kind to herself.** From around the age of about eight, girls can start to give themselves a very hard time for saying or doing the wrong thing. First, tell her not to be so tough on herself – and tell her how you, as an adult, have also made mistakes. But also help her heal herself if she feels she has done something wrong. Tell her to replay a painful memory in her head, and imagine herself as her own best friend, going up and giving herself a hug. It's sounds sickly, but it's a powerful way for her to visualise self-acceptance and self-forgiveness.

🗶 **Give her permission to love herself.** By the same token, little girls are told to love their mummies, daddies, siblings and pets – yet we often forget to give our daughters permission to love themselves too. Tell her that being her own best friend doesn't make her big-headed – it just makes means she's looking out for herself.

🗶 **Explain self-respect.** Teach her that self-respect means thinking of yourself highly, not because you're stuck up, but because you know and appreciate yourself deep down. Explain that if she constantly puts herself down, people won't like her more for it. They will take her at her word.

🗶 **Brainstorm how to work out problems.** Don't pretend you have a magic wand that will fix her feelings. Get her thinking about how to approach a dilemma herself. Our girls know the environment they are operating in best, so ask her questions about what she thinks the best approach is. More often than not, deep down she knows the best way to tackle it – she just hasn't been able to think it through or put it into words. Get supportive older siblings involved to give the benefit of their experience.

Teach her brain chemistry

Considering that the brain forms who we are and what we think, it is remarkable that we spend so little time thinking about how to make it work for us. So teach your daughter a bit about her brain and how it works.

Explain that there are only four basic emotions – joy, sadness, anger and fear – and everything is a cocktail of these. Tell her that each one is useful in its own right, and it's fine to express all of them, even if the negative ones can feel frightening. Then tell her about the brain's amygdala – a primitive structure designed to respond to threats – which can set off irrational outbursts particularly easily in the adolescent years. Talk about how the brain makes 'angry' chemicals which can flood the whole body and affect heart rate and respiration.

Then, show her how deep breathing can help bring her body back to normal. True explosions of fury generally last no longer than twenty seconds, and she will feel less frightened knowing that they will pass.

On top of all of this, hormones will play their part too. Make her aware that during puberty, hormonal changes may make her feel more emotional, but they are there to help her grow up. Mood swings can also sometimes make it hard for her to make good choices – so it's often a good idea not to rush into big decisions.

Once she recognises these influences on her mind and mood – even at this most basic level – your daughter will start to feel like she is in charge.

WHAT YOU CAN DO

※ **Explain how looking after her brain can make her feel more balanced.** Before the thought of dieting even crosses her mind, explain how 'brain foods', unlike junk food, will 'feed' her brain, boost how well she concentrates at school and improve her mood. Further down the line when she becomes weight conscious, it may help her see that dieting – and letting her blood sugar levels rollercoaster – will only make her feel miserable.

※ **Get her to recognise moments of joy.** Help her to seek them out and relish them – however she finds them. Most often they are found in the simplest things, like dancing or spending time in nature.

DON'T SAY 'NEVER MIND'

As I chatted to another mother at a play-date one afternoon, she dropped into the conversation that her seven-year-old daughter had been having trouble sleeping, and was then getting anxious about waking up for school the next day. The child, who was listening in on the conversation, joined in and was trying to explain that the chiming of a clock downstairs and anxiety about getting up on time in the morning was keeping her awake. Now that the child wanted to elaborate, the mother repeatedly told her – in a tone which made it clear she wanted her to be quiet – 'Never mind, darling. It really doesn't matter.'

The look of bewilderment as the little girl tried to express how she felt, and her mother dismissed her feelings, was sad to see.

Children need to be allowed to express the things that frighten and concern them – even if they are inconvenient to us as adults and stand in the way of us being seen as 'perfect' parents. By trying to portray ourselves as beyond reproach and viewing any problems our children are having as a slight on us, we are not being fair on them. Saying 'never mind' takes away the tools our youngsters have to recognise, name and deal with their emotions. If you tell them their feelings don't matter, or they've got them wrong, they stop trusting themselves.

Equally, if our children learn that their feelings make us uncomfortable, they are also likely to drive them underground. One of the reasons young people may self-injure is that their emotions are dismissed as wrong or inconsequential within their families. Self-harm or eating disorders become their way of expressing what they have no other outlet for.

So, acknowledge your daughter's feelings. Assume they are real. Let her process them, however trivial you consider them. We can't bully children out of their worries, but listening allows them to be brought to the surface, where they can be dealt with and processed.

PRETENDING THE WORLD IS PERFECT

Of course, it would be wonderful if we could make the world perfect for our daughters.

But despite our best efforts, it's never going to be – and we need to prepare them for this undeniable truth. Sugar-coating the world with a Disneyfied version of life – complete with a handsome prince who will sweep them off their feet – will only set up them for a life in which they will feel as if they have failed.

Be fair and truthful. Prepare girls for the fact that there will always be good days and bad days. Show them how, if they take responsibility for decisions and are truthful with themselves, generally the good days will outnumber the bad. Of course, some parents understandably take the view of: 'Oh, she doesn't need to know that.' We may fear that understanding how the world works might make children precocious or 'knowing'. But in reality, that's more likely to happen if your daughter takes on an inappropriately adult persona *without* understanding the influences at work on her.

Redefining intelligence

Our schools have the highest number of exams and assessments in the world. But not everyone can be top of the class – and for many girls in today's competitive society, this can be a blow to their self-worth. Unless we step in, it doesn't take long for our children to identify themselves as losers at life if their academic results are not sparkling.

Thankfully, times have moved on from the days when I was at school, and you were deemed either 'brainy' or 'thick' depending on your marks. The work of Robert Sternberg and Howard Gardner has turned that idea on its head by coming up with the theory of multiple intelligences. They found that traditional ways of measuring brainpower are much too narrow and don't take into account all the many different types of skills that develop in the brain.

So, tell your child there are lots and lots of ways to be clever, and recognise the unique jigsaw puzzle of strengths she has – including those that aren't necessarily recognised in classwork. To a child who is not top of the form in traditional subjects, the fact that brainpower is now seen to be a unique combination of all these different kinds of intelligence can be deeply reassuring.

The strengths your daughter has might include interpersonal intelligence (the ability to read and understand others) and intrapersonal intelligence (the ability to understand yourself). Talk to your daughter about people you know with 'street smarts', but not necessarily glowing exam results, who have done well in life, and about how the application of perseverance and determination will always take you far.

Furthermore, rather than letting your child believe that intelligence is something she can do nothing about, put the ball back in her court. Help her find her learning style. The three main learning styles are visual (seeing and reading), auditory (hearing and speaking) and kinaesthetic (learning through doing). Ask her teacher to test which style works best for her so you can help her learn more easily.

Explain to your daughter in simple terms how electrical signals make connections between the nerve cells so they form a network. The more the linked cells are used, the stronger the network becomes, forming a memory and eventually a skill.

Tell her that all brains are different and work in slightly different ways. Remind her that no one is good at everything – even Einstein had his limitations.

HOW TO HELP YOUR DAUGHTER FIND OUT WHO SHE IS

Finding your daughter's 'spark'

A spark is something that every child has – it's the thing they are naturally good at and just love doing. The concept, which sounds deceptively simple, was developed by the late youth development worker Peter Benson. He explained: 'Every child has a spark – something that is good, beautiful and useful to the world … A spark is something that illuminates a young person's life and gives it energy and purpose.'

Sparks can be musical, athletic, intellectual, academic or relational and consist of anything from helping to save animals, playing an instrument or a sport or growing and making things. They are split into three types: a skill or talent your child is naturally good at, a commitment such as volunteering or helping the world, or a quality of character, like empathy and being a good listener.

A spark is always linked to an innate talent because kids like to do things that come easily to them. Finding their spark helps youngsters use their time better and feel good about themselves. It can be used to help your child become more whole, better choose how she uses her time and might even eventually light her way to a fulfilling career.

To discover your daughter's spark, all you have to do is ask her what she loves to do. Eight out of ten twelve-year-olds will already have a good idea straight away.

But if your daughter is still too young to work it out for herself, watch how she plays. Keep an eye out for the activities which totally absorb her and which she will do when she is alone. That feeling of competence will carry over into other areas where she is less confident.

WHEN YOUR CHILD'S SELF-ESTEEM IS SUFFERING THROUGH LACK OF FRIENDS

It's heartbreaking for a parent to watch their daughter having trouble making friends, and it can be devastating for a girl's happiness. Even relatively mild communication problems can have serious effects on feelings of self-worth at a critical time. Children who feel unpopular are more likely to be depressed and get involved in risky behaviour as they get older.

At the age of nine, Victoria is the type of child that the other girls in her class describe as 'weird'. There's something about her body language and the way she 'hovers' at the edge of their games – but doesn't join in – which makes them uncomfortable. From time to time, Victoria also pipes up with 'funny' things at unexpected times in lessons – the last time was when she talked about where she went on holiday in Maths class. Behind her back, although never to her face, the other children complain too that Victoria is a 'show-off' because she talks 'at' them instead of just joining in their conversations.

Whereas traditionally child psychologists only really looked at how learning difficulties affect schoolwork, more and more they are looking at how it affects how well children fit in socially. Children like Victoria are often viewed by other kids as stuck-up, bossy, overbearing or 'geeks'. Until recently, it had always been assumed that communication and making friends is something that kids do naturally – even if some are better at it than others.

But now, for the first time, child specialists are looking at the possibility that not knowing how to make friends is just as much of a learning difficulty as conditions like dyslexia.

In the same way as those learning difficulties affect how well kids do at school, child language specialists now believe that a delay in the way a child's brain processes social cues affects how they get on with their peers.

Just as dyslexic children struggle to form words out of the jumble of letters in front of them, children with social learning problems – now known as dyssemia – can't read the right messages from facial expressions and body language.

For an ordinary child, it takes an average of three seconds to work out social cues. The brain of a child with dyssemia may be slow to read these signals. They have problems working out how other people see them, and difficulties forming the open body language they need to join in a group, as well as difficulty judging how to say the right things at the right time. Many parents of children like this sweep it under the carpet, not knowing what to do. They may try to explain away their child's behaviour saying, 'Oh, she's just not very good in social situations' or 'Grown-ups love her … she's just too grown-up for kids her age.'

But the good news is that the brain is a very malleable organ, and the social skills that children need to fit in can be taught. In the same way as children can overcome academic learning disabilities, child communication expert Michelle Garcia Winner says awkward children can also be taught the social skills they need.

'Even if they don't get it by intuition, we can teach children how to be social detectives – to think about how others see them and to use their eyes, ears and brains to learn what is expected from them. Some children may just need more help understanding these concepts than others.'

WHAT YOU CAN DO

❊ **Explain 'social smarts'.** Tell kids in the same way that they can be smart at Maths or English, they can also have 'social smarts', which can be improved through practice.

❊ **Teach kids to be 'social detectives'.** Use movies, TV shows or commercials to give children practice guessing what the on-screen characters will do next based on their facial expressions and body language.

❊ **Teach them about body language.** Explain how it affects the way other children see them. For example, tell them they will need to turn the front of their body towards a group – and maintain the right distance – to let other kids know they want to join in a game.

❊ **Teach them about eye contact.** Explain that if they don't use their eyes to look at people, other children will think they are not being friendly. Tell them they need to 'think with their eyes' to work out the right social steps to be accepted and included by other children.

※ **If your child can't make friends, seek help.** Don't waste time thinking she will grow out of it, because peer exclusion can cause long-term damage to her self-esteem that's difficult to reverse.

Other ways of helping your daughter find herself

For your daughter to stand strong against negative messages, what she needs more than anything is a strong, unshakeable vision of who she is, where she has come from and what she has achieved. The good news is that it just takes an interested parent and a little time to show her how far she has come.

WHAT YOU CAN DO

※ **Show her how far she's come.** Children quickly forget how much they have learned – especially when they feel they still have a long way to go. Keep chronological scrapbooks showing your daughter her drawings and letters, starting from her first scribbles to her latest projects. Keep the albums separate for each child – and make each one just about them. I have kept a library of albums charting my daughters' lives. Every time we look back through them, we not only have fun, but their sense of who they are and how much they've accomplished is reinforced.

※ **Help her teach little ones.** Children positively brim with pride in themselves when they can pass on something they are good at to younger children. Helping smaller kids with anything from reading to music practice takes a child outside herself, and does wonders for her responsibility and maturity. It also reinforces her own understanding.

※ **Teach her family history.** Plotting a family tree, looking back at old pictures and talking about your heritage gives a sense of belonging and continuity that makes children feel grounded and part of something bigger.

※ **Help her to help others.** A major finding of the Children's Society report is that unselfish people are happier than people who are preoccupied with themselves. Start by getting her to sponsor a child in need or an endangered animal. Let her pledge her pocket money to a good cause, or give her old toys to the charity shop. Teach her early how good helping others can feel.

※ **Keep family rituals.** Mark milestones so your child knows you are recognising and welcoming her getting older. Give a child of sense of occasion about her birthday. This isn't the same as lavishing gifts on her. Let her know how important she is by spending special time with her on that day. For her first birthday as a teen, do something extra special, like taking her away on a small break, so you start those years feeling close and she feels accepted and special.

※ **Learn from your child.** Children delight in knowing more than we do, so pay your daughter the ultimate compliment of learning from her. If she's rehearsing a new song for her school play, learn the words and sing along with her. Ask her advice on anything from helping to plan the week's meals to choosing the ripest fruit at the greengrocer's.

❊ **Help her find something she can seek solace in.** Help your daughter find an activity into which she can escape, and which is separate from school and the pressure to compete. It might be a type of music she likes to listen to or an absorbing craft or skill which gives her a chance to withdraw into herself and relax.

HOW TO BUILD
COMMUNICATION

'It's important that girls have times with their parents. I
just finished my exams and my mum took me out for hot
chocolate without my sister. We talked about friendship
and body image. I am glad she listens instead of lectures.'

KARA, FOURTEEN

When your child is being fast-tracked through childhood
it's easy to feel overwhelmed and unable to keep up. It can
be especially hard in the teenage years when your daughter may
not appear to give two hoots for your opinion – and seems more
interested in what her friends have to say. It's fair to say that unless
you take active steps to keep connected, this communication will
get much harder as she gets older.

Going back in time, remember how when your daughter
was a baby, you quickly developed a dance of communication
with her. Even before she could speak a word, you managed to
interpret what she wanted and needed. As she got older and your
little girl stretched out her hand to hold yours, yours was already
there to meet it. This dance continues through childhood, but can
seem to grind to a halt when your chattering eight-year-old starts
turning into a morose teenager, who doesn't offer you more than
an eye-roll if you dare to ask how her day has been.

But don't assume that because your teen is able to talk articu-
lately, she can automatically communicate her emotional needs.

At this age, girls simply may not have the words or self-awareness to explain what they are feeling. Sometimes as an adult, it's hard to appreciate how ashamed girls feel about feelings of worthlessness, and how much they subvert and try to hide these feelings behind moodiness. Part of the reason for that is that they are terrified of disappointing us.

All this means that as she grows you will need to give just as much attention to your child's emotional needs as you did when she was a baby. Looking ahead to when the times get tougher, you will need to build up all the loving respect you can earn – and get those communication channels firmly in place.

Dr Stephen R. Covey, author of *The Seven Habits of Highly Effective People*, calls this making 'emotional deposits'. These are good experiences that help our children know that we love them – and make them more likely to keep listening because they truly know that everything we do is for them. It means that when the difficult times come, as they inevitably will, our girls are more likely to hear us out and trust our advice, guidance and insight.

Especially as she grows more independent, there may well be days – in between your daughter coming home from school and you coming home from work – that you find yourself saying no more than a few rushed words. So it's more important than ever that you set aside dedicated time to be with her.

And if the rows and sulks find you dreading the sound of your child's key in the door, then it's definitely time to fix what's gone wrong in your relationship. At some point, she will slam doors, and she will call you every name under the sun. But through it all speak as much as is humanly possible, and in a way in which you would want to be spoken to. If you yell, she will simply feel justified in shouting back – and the really important messages won't get through.

Also try listening again. Is she really trying to push you away – or is she just trying to change the way you communicate by forcing you to recognise she is not a child any more? Most teenage rows are really about her insistence that you should start to acknowledge her as an adult. So prove to her that you appreciate how she is evolving. Be the grown-up that you are. Ask her to come and chat to you when you are making dinner, running errands or getting ready to go out. Look for every opportunity. But also set aside times when it's just the two of you, when you are just checking in to see how she is, and not nagging her about her schoolwork.

Take her for coffee or go to a museum together. Make it one-on-one time, when she has the chance to say things she might not otherwise have the opportunity to say. Make it casual and unforced, and skip lectures. Above all, let her know that she always has a voice – and that you are always, always on her side, even if she has things to say that you may not find palatable or easy to deal with.

Remember that girls are natural secret-keepers. Know that in the same way that you probably tell her only what you think she needs to know, she may also only be telling you half the story when she talks to you about what her friends are up to. For example, she may run scenarios that happen to 'friends' (but never her, of course) just to see how you react. It may be hard to get her to open up. Girls are so keen to present a 'perfect' image and do not want to let their parents down. But even if she paints just half the picture when she talks, she will feel better and you will be closer than you were.

By making it crystal clear she is entitled to make mistakes – and that you have made some too – and that you won't judge or punish her, you are getting a much more important message across: That she can always come to you.

At neutral times, explain that she will always feel better getting problems off her chest, even if she doesn't look forward to telling you. Tell her that you will only be able to help her get to the source of the problem if she's honest with you. You don't have to know the answers, but at least you've kept the conversation going – and given her your best perspective on the events in her life, so she can hopefully exercise good judgement.

And when she talks, listen. Like all of us, she just wants to be heard.

WHAT YOU CAN DO

For younger girls

❈ **Let her come up with conversation topics.** Find out **what interests your child and let her talk.** Try not to interrupt and give her extra time so she doesn't feel rushed or intimidated.

❈ **Go with the phases.** Are you secretly ready to scream if you hear one more fact about Frozen, or the subtle differences between every species of Moshi Monster? Bite your tongue. Know that it's just a phase and most will only last a short time. You will be paying your child the ultimate compliment. Even if you're secretly bored to death, see the bigger picture – that she wants to share her interests with you and that you are keeping open the lines of communication.

❈ **Share her enthusiasms.** Many phases will be more engaging for you too if you take an active interest in what she's talking about. Some of my children's happiest moments have been when I have sat down to play a game they love. By taking part, it will become less boring for you – and they'll feel great that they've turned you onto something they discovered.

❈ **Look at her when you talk to her.** There are days when we are so busy that we can go for several hours without ever truly looking our children in the eyes. Making that connection is vital. It shows we are listening and interested. Look up when your child enters the room. When they have something extra important to say, stop what you doing, look into their eyes and show you are really listening.

❈ **Keep reading to her.** She may well be happy to read to herself by the age of eight or nine, but that doesn't mean you have to stop. By reading to her, you are creating special time and staying connected. At a time when so much computer-based entertainment is available, reading can also allow her to explore situations and other people's emotional experiences at a more manageable rate – and with your guidance. Help her to find out more about herself by asking about the character's dilemmas and what she would do in the situation.

❈ **Talk in the bath.** Do you find the moment you take a bath, your daughter wants to join you? Often some of the best and most open conversations seem to take place when you're in the tub. Kids can relax because they can see you are not going anywhere – and somehow the water and the lack of clothes just seem to invite more honest exchanges than you'd get at any other time.

❈ **Use the quiet time before bedtime.** Another good time to talk is during the quiet time after lights out. In the same way that the water helps children relax, the darkness and lack of distractions also makes them more open about their real concerns.

❄ **Set up a mummy–daughter diary.** If your daughter is going through a phase of finding it hard to express her feelings, suggest a notebook which acts like an open diary between you, allowing you both to jot down your thoughts for the day.

WHAT YOU CAN DO

For older girls

❄ **Ease off the tiger parenting.** When the drive to help our girls changes from helping them to do their best, to making it clear they need to be THE best, girls can start to regard us as jailers rather than their biggest supporters. We may think we are simply helping them to do better, but many girls hear it as constant criticism, leading to a creeping sense of separation. Don't allow her to think you only love her for how good she makes you look, not for who she really is.

❄ **Be clear about how you feel.** As she gets older, some of the biggest misunderstandings will come not from how you treat them and feel about them, but how they THINK you treat them and feel about them. There may be a big gulf between the two. Leave her in no doubt about your feelings for her and how much you value her.

❄ **Keep hugging.** After our children are too old to carry in our arms, somehow many of us fall out of the habit of having so much physical contact. But sometimes a bad mood, a strop or a cry for attention can be cured with nothing more than a meaningful hug. It can feel much more significant than words. Scientists have found that hugging for just twenty seconds is enough to boost levels of the feel-good hormone oxytocin and keep kids up for the whole day. As teens become more self-conscious, find other ways to show reassurance and affection physically, even if it's just with a squeeze of the hand or a stroke of the back.

⚒ **Keep talking.** Even if you have said all the right things, your teenager may still appear to tune out much of what you have to say. But don't be discouraged. She is taking it in. Never let your clashes get so bad you start to view each other as foes. Tell her you are always on her side.

⚒ **Eat together.** A survey of British households found that 14 per cent of families never eat together because of the triple whammy of technology, TV viewing and long working hours. One study, published in the *Journal of Adolescent Health*, found that children feel more valued at family meals, even if they do not say much at the table, because they see the communication between other members of the family and feel that they are an important part of the unit. It does not have to be just dinner. Weekend brunches or breakfasts will work just as well too. Make it the rule that you will turn off the TV, put away your phones (have a basket to collect everyone's mobile – including yours – before the meal starts) and forget the lectures.

⚒ **Check your body language.** It's easy to assume that if we say the right words, our children will hear the right messages. But around 70 per cent of all meaning is derived from nonverbal behaviour. Even from babyhood, girls in particular are sensitive to every clue. Sighs, frowns and irritable body language are all picked up. So, instead of not looking up from your texts when she comes home from school, make sure your face really does light up, turn towards her and show you are pleased to see her.

❊ **Check your tone.** It's not just the words we speak that our children hear. It's also the tone in which we say them. One of the most hurtful tones is exasperation, which not only makes a child feel she is a disappointment, but that you have lost faith in her. Even if you are asking her to do something she should have done, or are repeating yourself, speak in a way you'd like to be spoken to. As in all human relationships, the key is how you ask.

❊ **Use humour.** Boys are much more likely to use humour to communicate, while girls tend to get highly strung. Some of the best parental communicators I know use laughter to defuse tension. The stress in our lives means that it's easy for the joy and fun of family life to ebb away without deliberate attempts to push back. Have family stories you retell. From a safe distance, find the funny side of things that have happened in the past. Develop in-jokes to keep you close, or watch silly videos together. Add silly emoticons to your texts so not every message is a nag.

❊ **Give your child a voice.** Organised family meetings are good because they address the internal dynamics within families. They can also allow girls to express anger with siblings – or indeed you – in a safe space where it's everyone's job to listen to one another. Don't worry if they don't happen on a weekly basis. Call them when you feel everyone needs to get a few things off their chest. Stay calm, don't sermonise, and listen, and you could be surprised by how easily they dispel tension in your home.

✂ **Don't punish honesty.** If your child is able to tell you that your constant comments on one subject are annoying her, don't take it as a slight or disrespect. Take it as a sign that she feels loved and valuable enough to express how she feels.

WHAT TO DO IF THINGS GO WRONG

With the best will in the world, our girls are still learning and, with so many pitfalls on the way, it's inevitable that your daughter will make mistakes.

The main reason that kids don't tell us when things go wrong, whether it's with their friendships or on social media, is because they think we, their parents, will just make everything worse. They fear we will use knee-jerk 'adult rules' and create a scene with the parents of any other youngsters involved, or storm into their school and cause it to become an even bigger drama that they will never be able to live down. Their other terror is that we will shut them off from their favourite websites and confiscate the technology which is the lifeline to their peer group.

When the worst happens, don't react immediately. If you find your daughter has been doing something you've always warned against, it's human nature to see it as an affront to your authority and to storm into her room with all guns blazing, demanding to know what the hell she was thinking. It may make you feel better in the short term, but this shock and awe response is exactly what girls fear most, and will stop them coming to you for help in future when a situation is slipping out of their control. So, first take a step back and give yourself room to process your worry and anger until you feel confident that you have sufficient control of your emotions to handle this situation calmly. If she comes to you – rather than you finding out another way – tell her you are grateful that she told you. Then tell her you are sorry that this is happening and that you will put your heads together to work out what to do. Later on, gently ask what thought processes led her to that action, so you can understand what has happened.

Don't shame her any further, share what she did with family and friends or hold her up as an example to other siblings. Allow her her dignity, or she'll never confide in you again.

Alternatively, if there's something that seems to be bothering your daughter that she just doesn't seem to be able to open up about, make yourself available and tell her whatever it is you are happy to listen and you won't get angry.

THE LITTLE MISS PERFECT SYNDROME: GIRLS AS THEIR OWN WORST ENEMIES

'I am fourteen and all the girls I know are already under a lot of stress. My parents and teachers tell me I can do what I want with my life and I've got so much going for me. But somehow to me, it just doesn't feel like that.'

SOPHIA, FOURTEEN

'Sometimes parents think they are helping, but they aren't. They are always telling you to do your best, but when you do, it's still not enough. If you get an A, they want an A-plus. As soon as you've passed your Grade 5 piano, they want to know when you're taking your Grade 6. I know they only want me to do well, but it feels it's not enough to be brainy. You have to be thin and pretty too. There aren't enough hours in the day.'

HOPE, FIFTEEN

'I've had parents in my study who've said: "I want my daughter to go to Cambridge to study architecture." And I've turned to them and said: "Lovely, but what does your daughter want?"'

JO HEYWOOD, HEADMISTRESS OF
HEATHFIELD SCHOOL

'Before she became ill she was incredibly driven. She was predicted As for her GCSEs and had won all these cups for rowing. As part of her depressive illness she has very low self-esteem, so while we on the outside can see she is stunningly beautiful – 5ft 10in, slim and gorgeous – she is not able to see that herself.'

ALISON HYSOM, MOTHER OF ELLA, FIFTEEN,
WHO DISAPPEARED FROM HOME FOR SEVERAL DAYS
IN 2013 DURING TREATMENT FOR DEPRESSION.
(Before her disappearance, Ella posted many references
to her appearance on Twitter, saying: 'Make me skinny and
I might start considering being happy with myself.')

Ever since girls started to outpace boys at school, parents have set the very highest goals for their daughters. While some will rise to the challenge, others will cave in under the pressure. Girls have always been more prone to perfectionism and, combined with the soaring expectations for academic success (which they internalise), this has led to the creation of a new breed of super-girl, dubbed Little Miss Perfect.

Bright as well as beautiful, Little Miss Perfect's exam results are as glossy and sparkling as her appearance. She is polite, responsible, loved by teachers for her perfect exam results and often has a social life to match. But we need to recognise that just because a girl is presenting this successful, high-achieving image to the world, doesn't mean she isn't still vulnerable.

Educator Rachel Simmons, author of *Curse of the Good Girl*, says that when largely middle class girls are asked to describe how society expects 'good girls' to look and act, they come up with these descriptions: 'The "good girl" was socially and academically successful, smart and driven, pretty and kind … She was also an individual who aimed to please, (people-pleaser), toed the line (no opinions on things) and didn't take risks (follows the rules). She also repressed what she really thought (doesn't get mad).'

As this description shows, this public veneer of 'good girl' can come at a high personal cost to a girl's real self.

If your daughter is obsessed with worrying how she looks to the outside world, she has no space to work out her own wants and needs. She feels unable to speak out. By trying to be perfect, ultimately girls doom themselves to failure. By setting the bar so high, a girl is likely to be brutally self-critical, eventually eroding her self-worth. She is so shaped by what she thinks she ought to be, she may put herself on an 'emotional diet' in which she only allows herself to express a limited range of feelings.

As Simmons says: 'Just as a girl might say, "I shouldn't eat this because it will make me fat", girls often tell themselves: "I shouldn't feel this. I am making too big a deal out of it. I shouldn't say this: It will make me a bitch, a drama queen, an outcast."'

The pressure to stay in line can become intense. If your daughter is prone to these beliefs, she may also feel that seeking help or taking her foot off the gas is a sign of failure she cannot admit to, and this can surface instead as eating disorders, depression and self-harm. Further down the line, it may also mean that girls never live up to their potential because they give up rather than stay the course when they cannot live up to their own exalted ideals.

This may be why, although there are more female graduates leaving our top universities with the best degrees, women are still underrepresented in politics, business and public life.

So, maybe what we need to tell our daughters is that they could do with having a bit more 'bad girl' in them. According to girls, a 'bad girl' is someone who argues, doesn't care about her body image, doesn't care what people think, has a tough attitude, speaks her mind and stands out – all qualities women of the future will need more than ever.

WHAT YOU CAN DO

- **Prize virtues other than obedience.** Early in childhood, we work very hard to train our children to do as we say. When they do, we tend to reinforce this with our highest praise, in particular telling our daughters they are 'good girls'. Girls, who are natural people-pleasers, tend to internalise this message more than boys. But as they get older they need to know they don't always have to conform.

- **Banish perfectionism.** As Judith Carlisle, headmistress of Oxford High School for Girls, points out, perfectionism is a fleeting moment, not a way of life. She says: 'In five years' time, no one will give a damn which GCSE grade you got in

French.' Remind your daughter that exams also don't give marks for character, persistence or creativity.

※ **Make sure your girl has a back-up plan.** Don't fixate early on just one or two high-flying universities for your daughter or make those goals the be-all and end-all. Otherwise, failure will feel catastrophic. Make sure she has goals in her life that are well within her capabilities as well as those that are harder to reach.

※ **Help her retrain her thinking.** If your daughter is showing signs of perfectionist thinking, suggest she poses questions to herself like: 'What's the worst that could happen?', 'If the worst happens, will I get through it?' and 'Will this be important next week, or next year?' Remind her that no one's perfect and she always has the choice to let some things go.

※ **Don't let her overschedule herself.** Help her to spot if she is doing too many things, whether it's playing too many instruments, taking too many exams or accepting too many roles. Help her find out what her spark is and help her use that to edit down her extracurricular activities to those she really enjoys. Encourage her to find activities that teach her life skills she can use for ever, like self-defence, meditation or yoga, rather than goal-led, competitive activities that only increase the pressure to perform.

※ **Point out that assertiveness and disagreement are not the same as being rude.** Show your daughter you can still be polite while expressing the opposite viewpoints and that being likeable is not the same as being silent or submissive. Point out if she is saying sorry before every sentence and tell her she has nothing to apologise for.

Repairing your relationship

Parents are often shocked when they wake up to realise how far their daughters have drifted away from them, even as early as the tween years. Often the sheer pace of life means they have not had the time to invest in keeping the lines of communication open with their children. Although parents are usually 'around', the breakneck speed at which we tend to live now means that girls process this busyness as rejection.

The first signs can start to show sooner than you think. Sensitive children who feel ignored, criticised or somehow not good enough will start to protect themselves by withdrawing. The first signs are often hypersensitivity, defensiveness or sulky behaviour. They may become less chatty and more secretive. Of course this all too quickly leads to a vicious circle in which they get labelled and blamed for being 'difficult' by parents who find it hard to admit they kicked off the problem.

If you have started to recognise that your child is reacting against you, first of all that's a huge first step. It is painful to face up to the fact that we are part of the problem. But your next vital step is to rebuild the connection and recover your empathy with your child that has got lost.

The first step is to let go of your ego, your personal expectations and any indignation that your child is somehow not repaying you by behaving the way you expect. Back down from trying to present yourself as a faultless parent and acknowledge you may have made mistakes. This does not make you weak in your child's eyes. Instead your daughter will appreciate that you care enough to find out what went wrong. She will be less defensive and more open when you acknowledge the fault is not all hers. Remember at all times that whatever has gone before, you are the adult with the experience and more developed emotional responses – and she is your child.

Undertake and stick to giving her regular one-on-one time so she feels secure in the fact you love her enough to reserve that space in your life for them. To kick-start that process, psychologist Oliver James recommends a technique called 'love bombing'. This involves spending a period of time alone with your child, offering them unlimited love and control over what you do in order to re-establish the trust between you.

James believes that by taking your relationship back to its roots, you can stabilise the levels of the fight or flight hormone, cortisol, which gradually keeps rising when a child feels rushed or criticised, and which may be keeping your child in a constant state of apprehension around you. The idea is that by freeing your daughter from being constantly controlled, it will take you back to the closeness and intimacy you once shared when she was a young child and any issues came between you. Of course, it sounds mad to give a child total freedom to set the rules. But it's only for a short space of time – usually a weekend – and children usually make perfectly reasonable requests.

One mother, Nat, who tried it said: 'I asked my daughter what she would most like us to do and she suggested a weekend at the hotel she remembered from a family wedding. We did a lot of fun things, like going bungee jumping and horse riding. I am usually constantly busy with work and always on my computer or iPhone. But this time I devoted all my time to my daughter and we had an amazing time.

'I noticed the difference immediately. I thought she didn't want to spend time with me anymore, but all she wanted was for me to tell her I wanted to be with her and make that commitment. All that sulkiness was a defence mechanism. It was as if we'd put a wrecking ball through the wall that had built up between us.'

HOW TO ANSWER THE TOUGH QUESTIONS CHILDREN ASK

More than ever we have to be honest with our children. The good news about our more open society is that topics which were once strictly off limits for discussion have now come out into the open.

Talking about difficult issues does not have to be as hard as we make it out to be. So many parents are so panicked about what to say that they end up not saying anything at all.

But if you want your daughter to be straight with you, you have to be straight with her. Remember, you don't have to have a magic solution. Don't lay down the law; just ask questions and help her think through the answers.

Yet parents still dread getting tough questions which make you feel like a deer caught in the headlights – like, 'Why can't I say bad words if you can?' or 'Did you ever take drugs?' As parents, there are plenty of questions that can leave us tongue-tied and fumbling for an answer.

Remember that when kids ask you about your experiences with sex or drugs, they are not really asking about you, but themselves. Gauge what they know first so you see how much they already understand – and what's age appropriate – before choosing your answer.

WHAT YOU CAN DO

⚜ **Think carefully before you speak.** Reflect the question back to the child and ask them what they mean by it to find out what's really on their minds.

⚜ **Let them do most of the talking at first.** Ask them what they think the answer is. Find out how close their guess is to the truth, and then just pause and listen. That way you will find out what question is really being asked.

⚜ **Make difficult questions feel normal.** Tell your child that many kids of their age have the same queries so they do not feel alone with their worries.

PART THREE

The Influences Around Us

So far this book has set out to put both ourselves and our
daughters in the strongest position to fend off messages that
could interrupt their healthy development. This third section of
the book zooms in on precisely what our girls are up against –
and exactly how we can train them to tackle it.

The Influences Around Us

PORNOGRAPHY

Growing up in a pornified society

'Even though my daughters are seventeen and thirteen, I have never had the "big conversation" about sex with them. If I did, they'd just raise their eyes to heaven, and say they know it all anyway. I just don't want to discuss that sort of thing with them.'

CELIA, 40

'I'm astonished that four- and five-year-olds are being brought to the attention of the police for sexual behaviour. It is another worrying example of sexual brutalising, and the internet is definitely contributing to that. It would be shocking if there wasn't a link between these offences and online porn.'

**JOHN CARR, FROM THE CHILDREN'S CHARITIES'
COALITION ON INTERNET SAFETY**

'I have an older son, and I was really disturbed by some stories I was hearing about some of the ways his mates were treating girls because of what they'd seen in pornography. So I brought it up one night with my ten-year-old daughter. First, I asked her what she'd seen, and she told me she was aware of 'nasty pictures'. Then I explained that whatever those nasty pictures were, they have nothing to do with making love. I told her porn is an industry which aims to shock you into wanting to see more so you spend money on it. She may

have felt a little embarrassed at the time, but underneath
it I believe all kids want to believe in love and intimacy.'

SUSANNAH, 51

Because it's such a difficult subject, parents prefer not to think
about their daughters even seeing porn. When I spoke to families, even those with much older teenage girls, most maintained
that their children were 'not interested', hardly knew what pornography was or would tell them if they saw anything disturbing.

But, though it's a painful reality, we live in a day and age
where it's not a question of if our children will see porn, it's a
question of *when*. In survey after survey, when questioned by adults
who are not their parents, youngsters talk about high levels of
exposure. Most studies seem to agree that one in three kids have
seen online porn by the age of ten – and the age has been sliding
downwards. Interestingly, it's increasingly not uptight, moralistic
adults who say porn is ruining our children's childhoods; in the
latest studies, it's young people themselves.

To begin with, children don't go looking for porn. Often
it finds them. Among the younger girls I spoke to, many were
aware there were 'yucky pictures' out there and were anxious to
avoid them. Porn is so embedded in the web there are even hardcore animated versions of their favourite cartoon characters, like
Disney Princesses and Peppa Pig.

Most children first encounter it when they click on the wrong
websites or misspell web addresses. Or it finds them via viral
emails, pop-up ads, banners or hidden among YouTube videos,
or they are shown it on other children's smartphones.

By the age of thirteen or fourteen, however, many girls' curiosity can become piqued. When questioned, older girls tend to
admit to seeing it – and say it was either 'funny' or 'gross'. But

behind the dismissive attitude, older girls seek porn out to see what the fuss is all about, to make sure they don't sound sexually naïve among their peer group – and ultimately to get tips on what they think boys expect.

The problem is it's easier for parents to believe porn is not a problem. Without even seeing the material in question, it tends to be dismissed as 'a bit of fun', or something that has never done them any harm.

While most parents have not been able to avoid hearing how pervasive it has become over the last few years, I am still amazed by the insistence of adults who continue to declare it's nothing much to worry about, mainly because it's a 'boy thing'. They are missing the point that even if their daughters never see porn, their lives will be still be affected because their future lovers, boyfriends and husbands will have partly been raised on it. Part of this denial is, I suspect, down to the fact that parents simply find porn too painful to think about. In some cases, mothers may be frightened of raising the subject in case it brings up some difficult conversations with their husbands, who they may believe have also been watching it, according to one of the world's leading experts on pornography, Gail Dines.

But go there we must.

Even over the last three years, there has been a notable step up in the degrading way women are treated in online porn. They are often seen being subjected to body-punishing acts which leave them grimacing in pain and tearful with humiliation. The market has become so competitive that pornographers have had to find increasingly shocking images with which to lure the viewers who are actually old enough to have credit cards and will spend money to purchase still more of it.

Vaginal sex, no matter how graphically filmed in extreme

close-up (and totally stripped of the pubic hair that could obscure the view), is now considered boring. Instead it has been replaced by women apparently in distress, forced to gag on penises, getting their faces covered with semen, and being anally and vaginally penetrated by two, or even more, men. Women are routinely portrayed being spanked, beaten or tied up, or as if they were being raped.

In the light of how porn has changed sexuality, 'making love' – a term I grew up hearing in the seventies – now seems quaintly old-fashioned. The sex here is all about 'making hate'.

'Gone are the days of women posing seductively as they coyly smile into the camera,' says Gail Dines. 'Instead, we enter a world of sexual cruelty and abuse where anything that can be done to a woman to debase and dehumanise her, is sexualised and eroticised.'

'All the emotions and feelings we associate with love – joy, kindness, empathy, happiness – are missing and in their place we see contempt, loathing, disgust and anger.'

This presents a big problem – and it's nothing to do with free speech, morals or the liberation of women. Indeed, no one who sees females being treated as no more than convenient filling stations, and called cunts, sluts and stupid bitches, can reasonably claim women are empowered by this – unless they have been swayed first by profit or polemics.

But the overarching problem with all this is that when our children, who have never come across anything to the contrary, encounter this sort of porn, they don't realise they are watching fiction.

Porn has become the most powerful and widespread form of sex education today. There is so much of it – and so much of it is claimed to be performed by real people – that girls quite understandably assume it's what you do with boys, and vice versa. The sex that our daughters hear so much about – and feel so much pressure to take part in – is shown as violence that men do to women.

For young children, who are born with an inbuilt sense of right and wrong, these images are also deeply disorientating. Studies have found that it takes a lot to undo these damaging first impressions if children don't know any different. Even if seen by accident, brain scientists are finding evidence that these images cannot be forgotten. As William Struthers, associate professor of psychology at Wheaton College, Illinois, says: 'A typical story would be a young [child] who is sent a link to a website by a school friend as a prank. The website may have a perfectly innocent-sounding name and [the child] logs on. Even though he didn't give his consent, the child then sees images he didn't want to see. You can't "un-see" something. These images are not easily erasable and become almost tattooed on the cortex. It is a powerful shock to the system.'

'We found that research subjects were able to recall the first images of porn they ever saw in remarkable detail even though they could not remember images they had seen more recently.'

The impact is so profound, says Professor Struthers, because although the hypothalamus (the region of the brain which controls sexual development) is preparing the body for sexual maturity, the higher thinking regions of the brain are not developed enough to deal with viewing extreme sex.

'Children may feel aroused, but they don't know how to make sense of that. This creates a sense of unease that they have done something wrong. On top of that, 80 per cent will never talk to anyone about what they have seen. They don't get the benefit of adult sexual maturity to help process this information.'

Furthermore, to add to their confusion, many of the females girls will see in porn are identified as 'barely legal' – in other words, only just sixteen – in order to get around child porn laws. They are depicted as real teenage babysitters, cheerleaders and schoolgirls. The message that young girls receive loud and clear is that they are already objects of lust too, old enough to engage in any sexual activity going.

Even when they look away from their computers, they see porn rubber-stamped elsewhere, by pop stars like Rihanna, Miley Cyrus and Nicki Minaj, who have moved towards heavy pornification in their music videos. And, though it's a phase which will no doubt morph into something else, as I write, it is currently taking the form of these singers mainly presenting their gyrating bottoms to the camera as invitations for faceless sex.

Younger girls – mainly under the age of thirteen – will initially greet hard-core internet pornography with shock. A survey by the Children's Digital Media Centre found that a quarter of young people who saw porn initially felt 'disgust, shock or surprise'. Other negative responses were anger, fear and sadness. But children may also find these images arousing, leading to a sense of shame which makes them afraid to share their feelings with adults who could help them make sense of what they have stumbled across.

Nonetheless, like boys, girls gradually become desensitised as pornography becomes their online how-to guide. As they get older, the number of teenage visitors to porn sites climbs. Between the ages of fourteen to sixteen, four in every five children say they regularly access explicit photographs and footage on their home computers. Two-thirds view the same material on their mobile phones.

Porn advocates, usually the ones who make the most money out of it, like to argue that it expands our sexual horizons and empowers women. Other polemicists like to dismiss concern as 'moral panic'. But that's confusing fighting back the pornifica-tion of society for old-fashioned right-wing attempts to repress women's sexuality. This is not the same battle. Porn is not just a freedom of speech issue, it has become a public health issue.

The really nasty thing about the ubiquity of this material – and one that will affect our daughters unless we move to counter it – is that this pornified behaviour is moving out of the realms of the computer screen and into reality. It will affect the way girls will be treated by the men they have sex with.

Those, like teachers, who see children's interactions away from their parents are expressing concern about seeing rape games in the playground. Police are dealing with a growing num-ber of sexual assaults committed by children as young as four who are mimicking what they have seen on their computers.

Further along the line, psychologists are asking what it means for future generations when the young addicts who are sent to them for counselling have viewed porn from such a young age – and at such a critical stage of sexual imprinting – that they can only become sexually aroused by the most extreme practices.

Is this painful to talk about? Yes, it is. I don't like to scare parents, but sometimes they need to be scared. If we stand by and say nothing, the ones who pay the price will ultimately be our daughters when they believe this is the only way to be sexual. No parent ever would have wanted to create a world where we'd have to explain pornography to primary school-age children, but if we don't, we are colluding with a billion-dollar empire that is stealing our daughters' right to a healthy sexuality.

So, as a mother, no, I didn't enjoy telling my daughters about what's out there – and how it might affect them. But I knew I had to find the right words, because the consequences of saying nothing would have been much worse.

How to talk to your daughter about porn

'Looking back now, I wish I had been told what porn was, so I knew to avoid it, and how empty, insecure and degraded watching would make me feel. I wish too I had been told it was not reality and that it's acting. I wish someone had told me that other girls watch it too so I didn't think I was the only one.'

BETHANY, 21, WHO STARTED WATCHING PORN AT THE AGE OF ELEVEN AND BECAME ADDICTED WHILE AT UNIVERSITY

If we leave talking about porn to our girls' teen years, we've already left it too late.

So many of the mums I have spoken to brought up the conversation with older children, only to find their girls had been exposed to it long before.

Think of this conversation as giving your child a shock-absorber for life. Don't be afraid that raising the subject will plant ideas in her head because little girls naturally dislike the idea of unpleasant pictures – and will want guidance to avoid them. Rest assured, there really are age-appropriate ways to discuss it. Remember too that older girls will hear about it anyway and it's always better to hear it from you. Consider that forearmed is forewarned.

If you are still finding it difficult to get the conversation going, that's understandable. I suggest you privately log on to any internet pornography site for just a few seconds and imagine viewing what pops up through the eyes of your child as if for the first time. I think you will find your resolve.

Or, listen to the views of young people themselves. Far from enjoying this free-for-all, according to the latest research by the think tank IPPR, eight out of ten eighteen-year-olds say it's far too easy to accidentally view explicit images. Seven out of ten said their childhood would have been better if porn had not been so available. In a separate poll, more than seven out of ten girls said porn had pressured them to look and act differently.

WHAT YOU CAN DO

For younger girls

❖ **Don't kid yourself that your child won't eventually be exposed to it.** Just because you're vigilant doesn't mean other parents will be. If your child does not see porn at home, there's still a good chance she will be introduced by her peers or their older siblings outside your four walls. That's why it's so important to keep the conversation going.

❖ **Keep it simple.** Explain that there are some things on the internet which are not meant for children – in particular violence and cruelty. If your child is still young, you don't have to specify violent sex, which is what most of this material now is. Tell her she will never get into trouble for showing you images that upset her.

❖ **Tell her what to do.** Teach her to tell a grown-up if she stumbles across an upsetting image. Another option is to download Hector's World Safety Button, an application which sits in the top right-hand corner of the screen and covers the offending image or message for your child until you come to remove it.

❖ **Support sex education in schools.** The organisation in charge of the online protection of children, CEOP, says that the age of first exposure to porn is falling all the time and that this needs to be explained to children in primary school. Even so, many families still baulk when they are told that topics like this will be introduced. Trust that schools are getting increasingly good at this type of age appropriate-guidance and appreciate the fact your child will hear it from a responsible source.

WHAT YOU CAN DO

For older girls

※ **Don't wait.** Don't worry that telling kids about porn will encourage them to seek it out. Studies from around the world have found that sex education by parents at an appropriate pace from an early age does not accelerate those interests. Instead, it makes youngsters proceed at a more measured pace. If you put it off, your girls will find out anyway, before you've put a buffer in place.

※ **Explain that porn is not sex.** Tell your daughter porn is not sex in the way that a thriller or action movie is not what happens in real life. It's like grown-ups play-acting for the camera and ignores the real purpose of intercourse, which is ideally to feel closer. Tell your girl that the happiest, most fulfilling sex, which both men and women enjoy the most, involves emotion and affection. Porn is created to make money, to shock and for the entertainment of the person watching.

※ **Tell girls not to compare themselves to – or feel they have to behave like – porn stars.** Many porn stars are surgically enhanced or picked for how rigidly they conform to an extreme caricature of the female sexual ideal. Many girls really believe this is what boys want and criticise their own bodies as a result.

🕸 **Don't overreact.** If you discover that your daughter has been watching porn, don't tell her off or she'll never discuss it with you again. Talk to her. Eighty-three per cent of teens don't talk to their parents about sex because they're 'worried about the reaction'.

🕸 **Explain the economic realities.** The fact is that porn is a money-making business. From talking to female addicts, one of the most effective ways they found to wean themselves off it was to learn more about the sex trafficking that goes on in the industry. Somehow this rational knowledge that other women are being abused in the making of this material helped them overcome the chemical lure of returning to it.

🕸 **Find videos to help make your point.** If you're worried your kids think it's just you, guide them to responsible, well-made videos that show that porn is a concern across society. Watch them first, of course, but try short clips on YouTube like 'The Science of Pornography Addiction'.

How to train our girls to deal with boys raised on porn

'I started viewing porn at eleven, so by the time I was at college, I had viewed literally thousands of hard-core videos of the most extreme kind: clips which stripped people of their dignity, in which women were passed from one man to another, were degraded by having men come in their faces.'

'Having started on porn so young, I had grown up with the idea that girls were objects I could use to act out what I had seen on the web. My main concern was not their characters, but how they looked. As soon as I lost my virginity at sixteen, I compared every girl I slept with to the girls I'd seen on porn. I'd openly joke about them with my friends if their bodies didn't live up to my ideals. I never met much resistance about the things I'd ask them to act out. Girls seemed to know what they were expected to do and felt they had to go along with it.'

'Among my friends, it became a challenge to see how much we could get girls to do in order to brag about it after. Considering how I'd learned about sex, I was rough and uncaring. All of us had naked pictures of girls which we would tell them we would keep secret but which we would automatically share with our mates. I got to the point where I could not look at a woman without imagining her performing a sex act on me.'

'The reason I went public about this is that I am scared for the daughters and sisters who are growing up with men who behaved the way I did.'

JONNY, 26, A GRADUATE WHO RECOGNISED HOW PORN CHANGED THE WAY HE TREATED WOMEN

'A lot of boys my age don't mind admitting they watch it, even though it can be violent. Sometimes I see it when I go round to my friends' houses and their parents aren't around. It's just boys. I think it affects how boys feel about girls. A lot of my mates get horny watching it and want to find a girl to do it with in real life, so some of them lose their virginity earlier. They think girls are just their boobs and arses. They don't think about their

personalities. They just want to act out what they see for real.
They pick girls up, use them for sex and drop them like toys.'

LUKE, ELEVEN

'All young boys are naturally curious about sex, but porn
amplified those feelings for me. I was turned off by a lot
of the more extreme pornography, but some of the older
guys when I was at school enjoyed that extreme material.
It's hard to tell who's going to be scarred by it. For me,
good sex is about knowing the other person's body really
well, not about feelings. Love has nothing to do with it.'

CION, SEVENTEEN

Times have changed. Not so long ago, or before the distribution
of porn on a global scale at any rate, it was generally thought a
good idea for a couple to know each other before they had sex.
In the scenario idealised by society, two people developed feelings for each other and then sealed those emotions with the most
intimate act of physical bonding possible: they made love.

We are now raising the first generation who all too often have
sex with people they have no emotional attachment to, and sometimes don't even like, and for whom the idea that you should use
intercourse for anything other than physical gratification seems
quaintly old-fashioned.

Sexually, although not emotionally, it is our sons who tend
to be the short-term winners in this equation. For boys, porn has
created a landscape where increasingly girls feel they have to offer
anything and everything sexually, in return for very little. When I
speak to boys who have used porn heavily, they describe the opposite sex less as human beings and more as props with which to play
out scenarios they have seen, and been turned on by, on screen.

The central problem here is that 90 per cent of the top rated porn sites these young men are looking at contain material portraying aggressive acts. A study by the University of East London of boys aged twelve to fifteen found that 97 per cent of those who had seen porn via a simple Google search were accessing scenes of staged rape, gagging and beating. Boys who have been aroused again and again by this sort of material tend to become turned on by fantasies of women as objects on whom they can perform punishing sexual acts accompanied by verbal abuse.

Furthermore, porn is also being used to force the door open to sexual activity before girls are ready. Girls engage in intercourse and oral sex without any promise of a relationship in order to appear worldly and in control. They may also go along with it because their confidence in their appearance has been so undermined by these messages that they seek out male attention to make them feel attractive.

Beyond the emotional hurt, there is also the physical hurt. Should we be surprised that pornography is now recognized as a factor in the growing number of cases of sexual violence against women? Sexual assaults have always existed, but they are not only becoming more plentiful, they are also becoming more brutal.

Sociology professor Gail Dines has interviewed thousands of men and women about sex and pornography. She says: 'When you interview young women about their experiences of sex, you see an increased level of violence: rough, violent sex. That is directly because of porn, as young boys are getting their sexual cues from men in porn who are acting as if they're sexual psychopaths.'

Porn works as an insidious two-way street. It's highly likely that by the time your daughter is having sex herself, she will have seen porn. The fact she has viewed it will mean she is more likely to do what boys ask, even if makes her uncomfortable, degraded or it is physically painful – because she thinks that's the deal.

Even adults feel they have to play up to the porn stereotypes. Studies show that more than one in five women feel they need to do more in bed to maintain their partner's interest, with one in seven feeling pressured to play out scenes that their partner has viewed on X-rated websites. If even mature women feel swayed, imagine how hard it is for a young girl tentatively trying out her first sexual experiences.

Indeed, anal sex and fellatio, now the favourite on-screen practices, which by their very nature tend to pleasure the male more than the female, are the real reason that teen pregnancy rates are falling in this country, not the fact that teens have suddenly turned sexually conservative, as has been claimed. As a result of this imbalance, doctors are seeing young women who have never had an orgasm because they have never had an intimate relationship with a partner who cared enough to give them one.

The hard truth is that we need to tell our daughters how pornography can affect the way boys and men might treat them, because without some perspective – even if that means being nostalgic – they won't work this out for themselves. Otherwise, the upshot of all this unbalanced sex is profoundly depressing, literally. Adolescent health specialist Dr Meg Meeker has suggested that depression in teenage girls may often be 'a sexually transmitted disease'. Researchers at the University of North Carolina at Chapel Hill have also reported that girls who engage in sex early are more likely to become affected by low mood than boys.

As media commentator Melinda Tankard Reist points out, fighting back against porn 'has nothing to do with shaming girls for sexuality. It is about naming a culture that teaches them that sexuality is all they are and sells ideas of sexuality back to them in distorted and harmful ways.'

WHAT YOU CAN DO

❋ **Bring back love.** As one teacher told me: 'Sex isn't a big deal anymore in the same way it was in our day. Young people don't even think they have to be in a relationship.' It is not misty-eyed nostalgia to point out girls are missing out if love and sex are no longer connected. It sounds obvious, but remind her she is much more than a female body to have sex with.

❋ **Focus on the emotional side.** Don't just issue dire warnings about sex, which will only make it sound more exciting and forbidden. Put the emphasis on patience, trust, affection and pleasure.

❋ **Ask her to take her time.** Tell her it's fine to keep talking about sex with her friends and finding out more, but point out she can't take back losing her virginity – and you don't want it to be a disappointment for her. Tell her sex is meant to be fun and intimate, not embarrassing and painful. Question if she wouldn't prefer to reach a stage with a lover where she can be open enough to say what she enjoys.

❋ **Ask her to make sure she is doing it for the right reasons.** Does she really want to have sex – or does she just want to be able to tell her mates? Explain that hormones, peer pressure and alcohol may all lead her to choose the wrong moment. If she really has found a boy she wants to sleep with, tell her to wait until she's sure none of these factors are influencing her decision. If he's the right one, he'll wait.

❊ **Tell her how porn affects men.** Explain how porn is changing what young men expect from young women and why. Tell her she has the right to say no to anything at any point that makes her feel uncomfortable, humiliated or used, and that if she is ever forced to do anything sexually that she says no to, this is rape.

❊ **Teach your sons.** Don't let your son buy into the rules of 'boyworld', like boys should not cry, a real man does not ask for help, women are not to be trusted and sex is a conquest. Instead, define a new type of manhood for him: being fair and equal in his relationships and emotionally literate. Talk to your boys about porn, the unrealistic expectations it creates and how it can alter the way males view females.

❊ **Warn her that porn is addictive.** Traditionally, porn addiction has always been seen as a male problem. But research has found that not only are one in three visitors to pornographic websites female, but a growing number of women are also finding it hard to stop accessing them. Females experience the same pattern of exposure, addiction and sensitisation to explicit images as males do. However, female addicts are more likely to suffer low self-esteem and depression because they have more difficulties reconciling their body's physical arousal with their dislike of violent, brutal acts that porn features.

A WORD ON FILTERS

A few years ago, it was hoped that filters could offer a simple fix for the problem of children seeing porn on the internet. But even if you have your own home locked down, on average, older children who are curious now have many different ways, from phones to tablets, to access the web – so there is no easy catch-all solution.

Nevertheless, filters still have a useful role to play. Apart from keeping violent porn out, they help to head off the possibility that your daughter could get led down the route of pro-anorexia or self-harming sites, which require time and opportunity to get deeply involved with. There is also a lot of talk about kids wanting to beat filters. But not all do, by any means. If anything, many children want to be protected. According to a recent study, 16 per cent of children know how to beat filters – but only half of that number actually decide to.

The other good news is that over the last few years, filters have become increasingly easy to install on phones, computers and search engines, so it's often a much less daunting task to turn them on than you think. Make it a blanket rule that as soon as the latest gadget comes out of the box – whether it's a laptop, tablet or new phone – you spend a few minutes switching on the safety features before you hand it over. Make it a strict condition of use that your youngster never attempts to bypass filters – and that you reserve the right to check they are still on further down the line.

POP VIDEOS

The pornification of pop

At the time of writing, the video for Nicki Minaj's latest song, 'Anaconda', has just been released – and it has all the hall-marks of what we've come to expect from today's pop promos. Stockings and suspenders: tick. Simulated sex: tick. Sensuous eating of banana and suggestive wiping of cream from lips: tick. Gyration of the buttocks: tick.

Indeed most of the video is gyration of the buttocks, which Minaj claims is evidence of her growing body acceptance.

With this video, Minaj has entered even further into hard-core porn territory, just pulling ahead of her closest rival Rihanna, whose main offering in her video 'Pour It Up' was also her pulsating behind. After several years in which female stars have competed to produce the most extreme videos possible, Minaj garners little in the way of shock, though it did attract 157 million views in the first month.

Far from being about female empowerment, explicit music videos have become about one-upmanship in an X-rated battle between many of the biggest selling female artists to see who can push the boundaries the furthest. No matter, how successful you are, the message is clear: if you're competing in this world and you are wearing anything more than a bra, pants or buttock-skimming shorts, you look seriously overdressed. Any clothes that are worn are fetish chic – sky-high platforms, thigh high boots and corsets.

Because it's all set to a beat, pop videos are one of the most mainstream ways that these sexualised images enter homes and slip under the radar of parents at all times of the day and night. Some will say that every generation tut-tuts at the music of its youngsters. Since Elvis Presley performed his first hip thrust in the fifties, music and sex have always been inextricably linked. Somehow because it's 'rock 'n' roll', video makers these days use this get-out-of-jail-free card to get away with more. But really they don't deserve to. They can't claim they don't know what they are doing, because their biggest consumers are young people.

It's also the relentlessness of these images that is problematic. A study of MTV's content by the Parents' Television Council in America found 1,548 sexual scenes containing 3,056 depictions of sex or nudity in just 171 hours. Raunch is also being used by the record industry to flog its increasingly flimsy products. While images of Minaj lap dancing in front of a fixated man nailed to his seat are seared into our minds, we'd be hard pressed to hum the tune that goes with it. Indeed, music and porn have merged so seamlessly that in one experiment, members of the public shown stills from music videos and others from hard-core porn couldn't tell them apart.

It is often claimed that our children don't understand what they're seeing. But you only have to see a group of nine-year-olds shimmying at a school disco to realise they get the message loud and clear. According to a Netmums survey of 1,500 parents, 82 per cent of their children had repeated sexualised lyrics or copied provocative dance moves. Look on YouTube and you will see hundreds of clips of toddlers and young girls miming the explicit words and movements of their musical heroines.

These songs have also become the soundtrack to their school discos, school concerts and birthday parties. When my elder daughter, Lily, then eight, sang with dozens of other school choirs at a cancer charity fundraiser at the Albert Hall, one of the numbers she was asked to sing was 'Bad Romance' by Lady Gaga, which included the words 'Let me take a ride on your disco stick'. She may have been left puzzled by the connotations, but it says a lot about the normalisation of this state of affairs that not a single teacher questioned the wisdom of such a choice.

Because these videos can be seen on any channel at any time of the day or night, the UK Government has now stepped in by giving music videos film ratings. But ultimately, it's up to parents to make sure we abide by them and help our girls develop the critical faculties to judge for themselves. Even if we are becoming desensitised to it, the fact remains that porn-pop has become the officially sanctioned version of the same pornography which teaches boys to think of girls as little more than rumps on a plate ready for sex at a moment's notice.

WHAT YOU CAN DO

❊ **Set limits.** Explain to girls that just because rude lyrics are set to music, they still mean something and it doesn't make it OK to sing them.

❊ **Turn off the X-rated soundtrack.** Of the many sets of influences raised here, music videos are the easiest to edit out. Don't leave video channels on all day and set your teen's parental controls on the computer to stop them getting streamed. Ask entertainers not to play inappropriately sophisticated music at children's parties and discos.

❊ **Watch videos with them.** With older girls, point out that, with the odd exception, women in the videos of male artists are mostly shown as sex objects and decoration while men are usually shown as powerful and in control.

❈ **Offer better musical role models.** Instead of letting them grow up on a diet of scantily dressed, manufactured girl bands, try introducing music by strong, independent singer-songwriters like Adele, Kate Bush, Annie Lennox and Bjork.

❈ **Explain the commercial pressures.** Discuss with older girls if performing in a sexually provocative way is really empowering to these female artists.

PRETTY BABIES

Make-up and drawing the line between make-up and make believe

'A lot of girls spend break time applying their make-up in the loos. I find it maddening because the girls are always messing around with lip gloss and powder instead of listening in class too.'

MADELEINE, A SECONDARY SCHOOL TEACHER

'When my daughter came along after my son, I was so excited and I couldn't wait to do girly things with her. She was about six when she started to put bits of make-up on. It was fun for me too because I wanted a princessy girl. She likes it because she says people notice her more.'

CLAIRE, 34

'I like getting make-up on, getting my tan done and getting my hair done. I'd never put anything on Poppy that I wouldn't use myself. I think Poppy just wants to be like her mummy. I'm the person she spends most time with, so it's normal. She's not had a spray tan yet but she's been watching me get it done for a while and she's dying to try it.'

MELISSA BRADY, 21, ON HOW HER DAUGHTER POPPY, TWO, WANTS TO LOOK LIKE HER.

Today six-year-old Rosalie is playing a more sophisticated version of a normal dress-up game. With a sugar pink Alice band in place to scrape her hair off her face and turn it into the perfect blank canvas, she is recording her ten step make-up tutorial for YouTube viewers. So far 40,000 people have logged on to view her tips.

Rosalie is clearly intimately acquainted with all the cosmetic lines she uses. Holding up each product with the expertise of a home shopping channel presenter, she tells how the eye shadow she is using today is in the shade of 'Fishnet' from Urban Decay.

Rosalie is far from the only primary school-age child on YouTube applying cosmetics like a seasoned professional. Scroll down the suggested video list and you will find dozens of other little girls – some as young as three – doing the same. There is Hannah, six, who also advises fellow 'make-up junkies' on how to achieve the 'smoky eye' look. Meanwhile Emma, seven, shows off her special 'Valentine's Day face'. For older girls, there are also plenty of routines to perfect their 'back to school' look.

The sad thing is that, in spite of these little girls' most deter-mined efforts, this is far from being a pretty sight. While viewers log on to shower them with compliments like 'you're so cute', seeing small children applying full foundation on flawless skin and chubby cheeks is actually rather sad. It's so poignant because they are little girls already infected by the notion that however beautiful they are, it's not enough.

But then, of course, there is already a growing market in products and services to encourage little girls to think that way. It's a mini beauty industry that's also being fostered by the recent craze for school proms. At these events, which have filtered down to primary schools, girls get prepped and pampered all day by beauticians to be red-carpet-ready. Nowadays, though, there's no need to wait for a special occasion: you can attend one of the many salons now offering services for children.

The opportunities for beautification are offered in the aisles of the nation's biggest toy chain, Toys "R" Us, where girls of any age can start with cosmetic kits like the Fashion Angels Make-up Set for £9.99. There are also nail varnish brands artfully targeted at the new type of child, cynically referred to as 'the sweetly sophisticated'. At salons offering the Little Bu brand, eighteen-month-olds expectantly splay their tiny hands in readiness for mini manicures in a range of twenty non-toxic, washable colours – designed so mums don't have to worry if their little ones stick their fingers in their mouths. For their older sisters, there are brands such as Material Girl Beauty and Willa, which actively target the pre-teen market.

As recently as 2005, the average age a young woman began using make-up was fifteen. Creeping diva-isation means that age has now dropped to thirteen and is continuing to fall rapidly. Forty-three per cent of six to nine-year-old girls are already using lipstick or lip gloss, according to Experian, and 38 per cent are using hairstyling products. Mintel research has found that 27 per cent of girls aged nine to seventeen wear eyeliner every day of the week, and 16 per cent use foundation daily. More than half say their mother helped them choose their make-up.

As Joel Carden, executive vice president for Pacific World, one of the world's major beauty product manufacturers, explained: 'It's the first door to beauty for the next generation … These are real cosmetics with natural ingredients that will create return purchases and create a true beauty consumer.' 'It's a marketing haven', crows the cosmetic industry's own website, Fashion Industry Today.

But then again, what mother has not caught her little girl at her dressing table, daubing on rouge? Isn't it just a harmless game of dress-up, a natural way of seeing how it looks and feels to copy grown-ups? Haven't little girls always wanted to look pretty? Yes, but now it's been allowed to take up a major part of their time and energy.

It's around the age of eight and nine that little girls become increasingly conscious of their looks. They want to know where they fit on the catwalk of life. And when our little girls spend their time looking in the mirror searching for problems to fix, it doesn't take them long to find some flaws. Too early, girls are set on a lifelong path of dissatisfaction no cosmetic can ever cure. Research by the Dove Self-Esteem Project found that 27 per cent of girls feel under pressure to look beautiful by the time they are eleven. What starts as lipstick and mascara for a special occasion can quickly become can't-do-without items on a day-to-day basis. Make-up interrupts the wonderful unselfcon-sciousness that little girls *should* naturally have about their bodies. One mother told me that by the age of twelve her daughter never left the house without spending 40 minutes putting on her make-up in the bathroom first. 'The saddest thing is she comes out looking worse – because there's nothing really to improve on – but without it she feels she can't face the world.' Teachers too told me they are infuriated by girls spending their entire break times re-applying their lip gloss and eyeliner in the loos – and refusing to run around the playground because they might smudge their mascara.

But girls don't need help being pretty: they are already. By bombarding them with make-up, they quickly learn that 'pretty' means 'sexy', and they feel that that's something they have to live up to.

It's true that make-up may make our girls temporarily feel good about themselves, but only because they are made to feel they are not good enough in the first place.

WHAT YOU CAN DO

For younger girls

- **Don't make prettiness the most important thing about your daughter.** Yes, girls should be told they are attractive, or they assume they are not. But make it just one part of who she is, and acknowledge her strength, skills, intelligence and personality too.

- **Don't fall for the 'natural' spin.** Cosmetics manufacturers have worked out how to overcome parents' lingering doubts about whether it's a good idea to buy cosmetics for little girls by branding them as 'natural' and safe for young skin. Don't fall for it. This is about more than whether such products will bring your daughter out in a rash. The effects of make-up for girls go more than skin-deep.

- **Divert her attention from make-up into crafts.** There's no denying that many girls are interested in adornments, so channel her creativity for as long as possible into craft kits to make jewellery and loom bands. They will probably spend more time making them than wearing them.

- **Explain your reasons early.** Somewhere along the way, your daughter will be invited to a play-date or a party where other little girls put on make-up. Before they do, explain that while that may be what their friends do, each family has their own values – and ask her to question why she should need to wear it so young. Even if she plays along, you have helped her question if it should become the norm.

- **Never give your child nicknames based on appearance.** Even if you mean it affectionately, teasing about appearance can cut very deep into a girl's self-image. Girls I have spoken to who wanted plastic surgery have often told me that they developed complexes from family jokes.

❈ **Focus on the present.** Try not to fast-forward by speculating on how attractive your daughter will look as a woman. Instead focus on the here and now of her childhood.

ACNE

One of the very real reasons many girls become reliant on make-up is because they develop spots during puberty. At this particularly sensitive time, when they are trying so hard to present a 'pretty face' to the world – and acceptance is partly dictated by looks – it's no exaggeration to say acne can have a catastrophic effect on their self-esteem. The feelings – despair, hopelessness, mortifying self-consciousness – can cripple even the most confident girl. They can become isolated and depressed and unable to look in the mirror in the mornings, leading to feelings of self-hatred and deep shame.

It leads to a slippery slope of more make-up use, because the more concealer and foundation they have to apply, the more it has to be balanced with lip or eye makeup.

Yet while as many as 85 per cent of 12- to 25-year-olds suffer from spots, only 15 per cent seek medical treatment for their condition – even though treatments have come a long way in the last few years and the NHS take the condition far more seriously. So even if you think she's making too much of a fuss about a few pimples, listen to her concerns – and if they persist, think about getting medical help, as well as offering makeup advice. At this time of her life, your daughter really needs to be able to turn her face to the light.

WHAT YOU CAN DO

For older girls

❊ **Teach her that make-up is to protect her skin.** Re-direct her to lip balm instead of lipstick, and from foundation to tinted moisturiser with an SPF to send her the message that the best make-up protects and enhances, rather than covers and masks.

❊ **Don't let her see make-up as a quick fix or cure-all.** At neutral times, when you are not fighting over the issue, explain that real beauty comes from healthy, fresh-faced looks, best achieved by eating a balanced diet, drinking enough water and sleeping well. Everyone has unique features that they can bring out with make-up – but stress that cosmetics don't make you who you are.

❊ **Give her the bigger picture.** Teach her how standards of beauty have changed through the ages – and why. Tell her that women once used lead to give themselves white skin and used corsets to shrink their waists to eighteen inches. Show her how social pressures have tried to make women conform to looking a certain way, even when it was not in their best interests.

❊ **Don't model make-up-obsessed behaviour.** Avoid making comments about how you 'wouldn't be seen dead without your face on'. Don't run for cover if someone tries to take your picture if you're not fully made-up. Send the message that you wear make-up first and foremost to protect and enhance, not to make you look like someone you are not. Admire other women who go make-up free and show your girls you are happy to leave the house without a fully made-up face.

❊ **Let her experiment if she insists.** Understand that your daughter might want to experiment, but emphasise that she is still lovely without make-up. Show her old pictures of herself growing up to illustrate she looked beautiful before and will still look beautiful if she chooses not to wear it.

❊ **Guide her safely.** Some guidance on how to apply make-up can also be a good idea if she's dead set on wearing it. Teenagers often assume they need more than they really do. If she's often making herself look worse rather than better, consider getting her some advice at a cosmetics counter. She may feel the need to wear less if she's more confident about how to apply it.

❊ **Give her the commercial realities.** Discuss issues like testing on animals and the fact that there are concerns over some of the chemicals in make-up. Talk about how packaging is designed to seduce women to buy and point out how, ounce per ounce, make-up is one of the most expensive commodities in the world.

❊ **Ask for the school's policy on make-up.** It may not stop your daughter adding a slick of lip gloss on the bus on the way to school, but it will keep other parents conscious of the issue, and at least foster an atmosphere where it is not encouraged and won't take up too much of girls' time.

BODY IMAGE

'When I grow up I want to be thin'

'I saw that they had practically cut me in
half. So it was pretty mind-blowing.'

**MEAGHAN KAUSMAN, AN AUSTRALIAN
MODEL WHO SPOKE OUT AGAINST A
COMPANY THAT PHOTO-SHOPPED HER
IMAGE TO TURN HER INTO A SIZE FOUR**

'No matter what I do, or whether I achieve
the career I want, I feel I won't have succeeded
unless boys think I am "hot" as well.'

SHIMI, SEVENTEEN, SIXTH FORM STUDENT

'My daughter is 5ft 7in tall with a lovely face and beautiful
body because she is very keen on sport. You'd think there'd be
nothing anyone could pick on, but one day she came home
saying she was ugly. When I got to the bottom of it, one of the
girls had picked on the fact that one tooth was slightly longer
than the other. You'd have thought her world had caved in.'

ALISON, 41

'How much we weigh is one of our main topics of
conversation. We all take turns complaining about our
bodies and saying which celebrity's bottom or boobs we'd
like. Then we like to find out what diets they are trying
and give them a try. We are always trying to take thin

pictures of ourselves to put on Facebook. It's important to have a really good profile picture to get more friends.'

JOANNA, FOURTEEN

'All my life I have battled my weight. I didn't want my daughter to know so I tried not to say anything in front of her. But the messages still hit home. One day as I was ready to go out to a big event, she saw me looking critically at myself in the mirror. She told me: "You shouldn't worry so much. You look lovely." I wished I'd address my own body issues first instead of trying to paper over them.'

JESSICA, 41

'If my two teenage daughters really want to upset each other during a big row, they start calling each other "fat". That's when the big guns come out and usually one or both of them ends up in tears.'

CLARE, 48

Children begin to recognise themselves in the mirror at about two years old. It's a sobering thought that within a few years little girls (but interestingly, not yet little boys), barely old enough to write their alphabet, are already looking at their reflections and deciding they don't like what they see.

Half of three- to six-year-old girls say they worry about being fat, according to the British Journal of Developmental Psychology. By the age of seven, 70 per cent want to be thinner. By nine, nearly half have been on a diet. By the age of ten, one in ten girls is 'extremely worried' about becoming fat and one in four has tried dieting, according to a large-scale study conducted by the National Institute for Health Research. It follows that by the time they are between the ages of eleven and seventeen, being thin has become the number one wish in life for many girls.

Indeed, all too soon, instead of seeing their true reflections, girls become trapped in a maze of fairground mirrors – with a warped idea of what it is to be normal.

So, how do small children so quickly get the message that in this society, thin means success and fat means failure – and that a person's worth drops in inverse proportion to their weight? Painful though it may be to admit, the first lessons girls get about their bodies are at home, from us. Low-calorie, low-fat, high-carb, low-protein, gluten-free … considering food is such a simple and essential commodity, we've made it incredibly complicated. As girls watch us skipping meals, trying the scales, obsessing about weight and criticising our bodies, they quickly cotton on to the fact that food is a power-broker with the leverage to make their parents feel guilty and depressed. Food is always, always on our minds. Within almost every woman today, there is an ongoing conversation about how to achieve or keep our ideal weight – directed by nagging voices asking: 'Is it OK to eat this?' and 'How fat do I look today?' Considering that a recent experiment found that the average adult woman thinks negatively about her body image 36 times a day, it's hardly surprising our daughters pick up on this preoccupation – whether we try to hide it or not.

Even conscious mums who try to actively model healthy living and never ask, 'Does my bum look big in this?' can end up unwittingly sending out unbalanced messages that their girls pick up on. As Deanne Jade, founder of the National Centre for Eating Disorders, told me: 'Even if you think you are modelling good behaviour by telling your daughter you are going to the gym to get healthy, not thin, it can create the anxiety in a child that it's the only way to be healthy. Everything we say sends a message which can be much louder to the ears of a child. Leading a healthy lifestyle is not about modelling our own perfectionist standards. It's about modelling a balanced sense of self-care.'

It's a hard, cold truth, but as our child's first and biggest influence, we have to look to ourselves.

As the first generation to grow up where stick-thin proportions were admired (in the sixties and seventies), we were raised with the mantra: thin is good. Because for the first time in history, food was plentiful and cheap, skinniness became the new elite, seen as a measure of self-control and worth. And now we've had children ourselves, these ideals have passed into our daughters' heads as if via osmosis.

So when it comes to body image, we have to fight the battle on two fronts – against our own hang-ups and against the messages that bombard children from everywhere else. Otherwise our girls' right to enjoy their bodies for what they can do is interrupted throughout their childhood by worries that everything about them looks wrong.

WHAT YOU CAN DO

- **Ask her what pressures she feels under.** Find some opportunities to chat. Deanne Jade says: 'If my child told me she's fat, I wouldn't answer. I'd say: "What's worrying you? Come over here for a hug."' Ask her to write down her worries about body image, so she can see them in black and white. By externalising, she may be better able to see the pressures on her more clearly.

✤ **Pick your moment.** At neutral times – i.e. not at a time when your girl is insecure about her looks and it will sound as if you are trying to console her – explain that what makes someone an attractive person to be around is the sum of all their parts, not just their appearance. Praise other women for their strength and personalities.

✤ **Stop stressing about food.** A healthy child will never starve. Don't force, cajole, nag or demonise. You will be giving food far too much importance if you do. Make sure your home is stocked with a wide range of balanced foods and the rest will follow.

✤ **Help children realise that celebs don't look that good in real life.** Explain that, thanks to airbrushing and stylists, not even models and celebrities look like the images we see in magazines. There are also plenty of examples of shoots pre- and post-airbrushing on Google Images. Once seen, your daughter won't forget.

✤ **Listen to her.** Eating disorders are often the last resort for girls who are not being heard any other way, says eating disorder expert, Professor Julia Buckroyd. Overscheduled and under pressure to be perfect, they don't have a voice, so they protest with the one thing they do have control over – food. Make sure your child can really talk to you and that you hear what she is saying, not what you want to hear.

✤ **Talk about different body types.** Self-acceptance is a key part of developing a healthy body image. Talk about the fact that there are different body types that are laid down in our genes – and models just have the DNA that makes them tall and thin. Explain that healthy weight is different for every woman, based on her build and height.

❉ **Define a new type of beauty.** It's never going to be possible to avoid all discussions of appearance. Indeed, the grown women I spoke to whose parents never commented on their appearance filled the vacuum this created by assuming they were ugly. So some reassurance is necessary. Create your own definition of beauty by admiring other women outside the stereotype – and encourage your daughter to find hers. Don't labour the point, but let it be known that the easiest way to look good is by eating a balanced range of foods, getting sleep and being active in lots of different ways.

❉ **Explain the concept of being too thin.** If she seems to be impressed by extreme skinniness, tell her that being thin and undernourished is not healthy or attractive, and though boys may claim to like slimmer girls, in reality it's more likely they prefer normal, more natural shapes. Explain how being too thin is just as unhealthy as being too fat. If she admires a celebrity for her skinniness, remind her that although we can see her public image, she won't see the hunger, the time and deprivation that has gone into maintaining that look.

❉ **Don't judge others based on what they look like.** If you're constantly passing comment on what other women look like, then your daughter will also start to rate herself by your standards. When you talk about other people, talk about their positive personal qualities instead, like loyalty and kindness.

❉ **Emphasise bearing.** Tell her how grace, bearing and posture are the best ways to show off her poise and figure.

- **Challenge the critical voices.** Girls are being raised in a hypercritical culture, and they quickly learn to internalise these voices. They also feel that if they get the criticism of themselves in first, no one else can hurt them. It's a form of mental self-harm in which verbalising these thoughts feels both painful and liberating at the same time. If your daughter expresses reservations about the way she looks, listen carefully without dismissing her worries. Don't agree or say: 'You're fine.' Suggest that she wouldn't allow anyone else to say such cruel things to her, so why should she say these things to herself? Point out the fact that even the most famously beautiful women in the world have been known to express dissatisfaction about their bodies to show how this constant yearning for self-improvement is ultimately a road to nowhere. When your girl is old enough, explain that constantly criticising her own looks is like allowing the oppression of women to operate from inside her head. Tell her to reject those voices.

LOOKING AT OUR OWN REFLECTIONS

The cult of youth means that most of us spend a lot of time and money trying to look younger. As our girls turn into teens and try to look older, we all seem to be trying to reach an elusive no man's land of perfection somewhere in the middle. Fifty may be the new 30, but at the same time, has twelve become the new 25?

All of this means that even mature, adult women never give themselves a break. A study, published in the *International Journal of Eating Disorders*, found that 70 per cent of women over 50 are still trying to slim, and 62 per cent say their shape has a negative effect on their lives. Up to 10 per cent also develop eating disorders, like bulimia nervosa and anorexia nervosa, for the first time in later life.

The world is full of women like Janice, 45, who told me that she recognises how her own expectations of her looks have changed throughout her lifetime, and why.

Although no more than 48 kilos, she still decided she wanted to emulate Victoria Beckham and put herself on a strict calorie-controlled diet shortly after going through the menopause.

'When I was a younger woman, I looked up to celebrities like Liz Taylor. I idolised them. They were unattainable. But now the more you read about A-listers, the more possible it seems to look like them – and the more you think you should do what they do too.'

Psychologist Dr Cynthia Bulik, professor of eating disorders at the University of North Carolina at Chapel Hill in the US, also believes that body image issues have become a cradle-to-grave issue for women, most of whom will become mothers. Indeed, rather than growing out of such worries, she has come across grandmothers who see the upside of illness being that they lose pounds – and even welcome chemotherapy as a way to suppress their appetite. Dr Bulik even told me she found one 76-year-old woman who, when she realised her cancer was terminal, begged her daughter not to dress her body in a dress that made her look 'fat' after her death for her funeral.

During my research on body image, mother-of-two Sharon, an admin manager in her late forties, told me of the terrible toll that constant self-criticism has taken on her peace of mind.

'Even now, my body obsession is still with me. I need to know I am still attractive, so I constantly watch calories. The moment I wake up, I weigh up how many I can consume. It's like a constantly running tally in my head.'

Sharon was honest enough to admit that while her children were growing up, she repeatedly chided them not to gain weight because it was her greatest fear. Partly as a result, her 21-year-old son had developed bigorexia – a male compulsion to over-exercise, which compelled him to start exercising at 5am – while her daughter had become bulimic, just as Sharon had been since the age of fourteen. For Sharon, and so many others like her, this is a hard-fought battle with herself that she has been waging all her life.

But unless we start to face the influences weighing so heavily on us as parents, we risk being the magnifying glass that makes these worries loom ever larger for our daughters.

The flip side: What to say if your child is overweight

'When she got ready for a party we'd spend hours getting her hair and clothes just right. Then she'd ring twenty minutes later in tears and beg me to take her home because all her friends had turned up in miniskirts, which she couldn't wear.'

JULIE, 49

'I feel so fat and worthless and think that I will never be loved – I am just a waste of space. I feel like curling up in a ball and crying all the time. I starve myself as it's the only way I feel happy with my life and in control. I see skinny girls at school and on TV and they are tiny compared with me. I binge sometimes until I physically can't eat, and other times I will eat nothing for days.'

CHILDLINE CASE STUDY

We are living in a nation of two extremes. On the one hand, there has been a steep rise in the number of pre-teen children treated for anorexia and other eating disorders. According to NHS figures, hospital admissions have tripled in four years. On the other, we are told there is an obesity epidemic and 29 per cent of our girls are overweight or obese. The result is that our world has become a two-tier society in which the aristocracy are size zero celebrities, while anyone overweight is considered to be in an underclass. This all means that weight has become such a delicate subject in our homes that parents are frightened to raise the subject, even if the health and well-being of their daughters is at stake.

At the same time as we are told not to make food a cause of anxiety, kids come home from school lessons quoting government directives about carbs, proteins and fats, having been weighed and measured to find out where they sit on the percentile. It may be the elephant in the room, but the painful reality is that in this unhealthy environment, girls can be led down a path to dangerous levels of self-hatred, which not only takes up a huge amount of their headspace, but can have a long-lasting impact on their self-worth and stop them taking part in activities like sport.

Saying nothing is not the solution because it can have an impact on a girl's health long-term. Sixty per cent of youngsters who are overweight between the ages of two and four are still too big at twelve. Seven out of ten overweight eleven-year-olds go on to become obese young adults. But fear of triggering an eating disorder – and a desperate hope that it's just puppy fat that will drop off – means many parents feel like deer trapped in the headlights. In the process, mothers of overweight children told me they felt looked down on by other parents, and as if they had failed their daughters.

Let me stress right now that this is NOT about fat-shaming. If your child is genuinely comfortable in her own skin – and is the shape she was always genetically meant to be – then there is no issue to address. But if your daughter does not have a happy acceptance of her body and/or is unhealthily overweight, we need to intervene by helping her to take control of the situation, rather than leaving her to turn the feelings of frustration back on herself.

When children do put on excessive weight, they may lack the maturity to know what to do, bury those feelings and start to comfort eat or eat in secret, which only compounds the problem, making them feel trapped and hopeless. Deanne Jade of the National Centre of Eating Disorders says: 'There is no simple answer. Childhood obesity is not simply caused by parents feeding their children junk food.'

'Some children have a harder job managing their weight. Many have emotional issues that trigger problems. Yet the parents of fat children often end up feeling like bad parents. They know people are looking at them, thinking: "Why don't you put your child on a diet?" As a society, we have to appreciate how hard it is for parents to refuse their child an ice cream if their friends or siblings are having one.'

'Restricting food only makes it more desirable to children — and it's one of the things they rebel over — so it's hard for parents to get the balance right.'

So how should parents broach the subject? First, check your own attitudes. Is your daughter really getting overweight, or is she simply outside of your mental template of how you would like her to look? Is she actually bothered by it – or do you just think she should be? Remember too that it's normal for girls to put on 20 per cent of their body weight in fat during puberty, and they may put on weight before they have a growth spurt.

Often you may have to look at whether your family eating habits are partly responsible. Has quantity become more important than quality? Has food become what you 'do' as a family? Have junk foods become so plentiful in your home that they are the first thing your child turns to?

If you are certain your child has tipped the scales into obesity – and you believe it's leading to teasing and self-esteem issues that are damaging her, then steel yourself to gently find out how it's affecting your child.

Amie, thirteen, who started to going to a slimming club after her mum found the courage to say she wanted to help when she tipped the scales at thirteen stone, told me: 'Being a fat child is a lonely place to be. I used to cry on my own rather than admit to Mum what I was feeling. It's so good to have my mum on my side now. To any mum, I would say it's always better for your child to hear it from someone they love, like you, than from someone in the playground calling them horrible names.'

WHAT YOU CAN DO

✳ **Ask her how she feels.** Among the first signs that a girl is worried about being overweight is that she becomes increasingly emotional when getting dressed. She may lose her temper trying to find clothes that fit her, wear baggy clothes, turn down social invitations or blame you for the fact she has 'nothing to wear' because she's grown too big. Other clues are that she seems uncomfortable or sulky during shopping trips and secretive about trying clothes on. Remember that girls are often too ashamed to say why they feel like this, so give her lots of hugs and time, ask her to tell you if anything's bothering her, and let her know that you are there to help. Deanne Jade says: 'When the issue comes out, it's usually a huge relief for her.'

- **Tell her you are a team.** As soon as her worries are out in the open, tell her that she is not alone and you will work together. 'It's key not to be judgemental but supportive,' says Deanne. Don't set her apart, single her out or give her special meals. Instead, start exercising and cutting down on junk food as a family.

- **Tell her not to diet.** Diets are not the answer for children, but healthy lifestyle choices are. Explain that dieting does not solve weight problems; it often creates them, and 95 per cent of them fail. Tell your daughter to eat when she is hungry because eating well and regularly are essential to keep her mood balanced and to stop her feeling deprived. Emphasise quality, not quantity. Don't prioritise skinniness. Instead make the goal toning, muscle strengthening and flexibility.

- **If chronic overeating is a problem, get to the root cause.** Professor Julia Buckroyd says: 'Ask yourself: "Is this child unhappy – or bored? What's going on at school?" For children nowadays there are very few ways of registering distress except for bad behaviour and overeating.'

- **Take it slowly.** Help her to address the issue slowly and steadily so losing weight does not become an addiction. Consider attending a slimming club with her – even if you don't need to lose the pounds – to lend her support and help her learn healthy eating habits.

TACKLING EARLY PUBERTY

With her hair in bunches, Atlanta looked like any other happy-go-lucky eight-year-old when she started school in Year Three. But as her mother Emma told me, there was much more on her mind than play-dates and her latest favourite book. She had already started her periods.

'Atlanta was in the bath when I first noticed a few hairs, when she was eight years and three months old,' said Emma, who understandably thought that it was too early to bring up the subject of menstruation with her child. 'A few months later, they started.' Yet when she consulted her GP, Emma was surprised to hear that Atlanta's hormones were considered to be in the normal range for a child her age. In fact, as studies across the world show, the age when girls are physically maturing is falling all the time, and doctors are revising their opinions of what is 'normal'. According to official NHS advice, precocious or early puberty is only diagnosed if breast or pubic hair growth 'starts before the age of six to eight years of age in girls'.

And there is no sign that it is levelling off. Every decade, the average age for the onset of puberty falls by four to five months, according to German researchers. It means that some girls who appear to be growing up faster than ever, actually are.

In girls, breast development is generally the first sign of adolescence. The most comprehensive US research suggests that it starts in about 10 per cent of white girls and among 23 per cent of black girls by the age of seven – around double the number fifteen years ago.

So what is causing precocious puberty? Doctors are often unable to explain the phenomenon – but one theory is that exposure to chemicals which mimic the effects of hormones, and which are in foods as well as plastics, may be triggering maturity sooner. Other studies have linked it to the fact that girls are generally gaining weight earlier in life thanks to better nutrition, while others still have found a link to exposure to artificial light from TV and computer screens.

Whatever the cause, it means that parents – as well as primary schools – may have to be more sensitive to the changes their girls undergo, and bring the subject up a little earlier than we might have done a few years ago.

WHAT YOU CAN DO

✳ **Get her ready.** It can be unsettling for a girl who is going through puberty to be on tenterhooks about when her period will start – or to live with the fear that she might start bleeding in the middle of a lesson. If your daughter is showing the physical signs that her periods are imminent, give her a discreet pack of pads and a spare pair of pants to keep at the bottom of her school bag. Girls tend to imagine that blood will start pouring out suddenly and take them by surprise. But reassure her that it will start off as a trickle and she will soon learn how to manage it. Tell her your experience of your own first period to help her gain perspective.

❋ **Stay positive.** Present the start of her periods as something to celebrate. Take her somewhere special together so she knows that this is a special event, but that life afterwards will still go on as usual. In the same way that we can influence our daughters' view of birth, we can make them feel more positive about menstruation. Don't refer to it with terms like 'the curse' or tell her she can automatically expect to get PMT, because not all women get this, and some studies suggest this can implant the idea in the mind. Make it clear that even though her periods mean her body is ready to make a nest for a baby to grow inside her, it will be years before she will be emotionally grown-up enough for that to happen.

❋ **Prepare yourself.** For mums, the fact that the child who was only in the nappy stage not long ago now needs to change her own sanitary pads and is able to conceive a child takes a mental transition. Child psychologist Emma Citron told me that mothers find it easier to adjust if they separate the physical changes from their child's sexuality. 'It's important to keep the two things distinct in their minds. This is a physical thing. It's not part of being a sexualised person yet.'

❋ **Treat your daughter as the age she is, not how old she looks.** So often, we seem to take more notice of what we see with our eyes than what we know in our heads. Even if a girl looks physically developed for her age, emotionally she is still her chronological age. It's unfair to treat a girl like a twelve-year-old when she's still only nine. Remind close family, including dads and grandparents, of this, as it's easily forgotten.

❋ **Talk to the school.** Increasingly, primary schools need to be sensitive to the needs of girls starting their periods and provide sanitary bins, so early starters aren't singled out by classmates for having to use the staff toilets. Ask the head to make sensitive arrangements, and discreetly inform the class teacher if your daughter is still at primary school. Otherwise, do not embarrass her by making a fuss or revealing to others she has started her periods, unless you have her permission.

BRANDED

Resisting fashion and beauty advertising

'Whenever I open a fashion magazine, I feel fatter,
uglier and more depressed. But at the same
time, I can't stop myself picking them up.'

MIRIAM, SIXTEEN

One summer, when my older daughter was ten, I counted all the images of women she saw on her way home from school on the bus. In her half-hour journey home on public transport, I counted more than twenty. Most were partially dressed or presented in underwear. Some were images repeated several times over, but as I added them up, I saw that females in adverts in general wore 20 to 50 per cent less clothing than males.

The female form has been used to sell products since the Victorian period. Even portraits of queens have been prettified during restorations to bring them into line with changing standards of beauty. But where once billboards were full of stereotypical domesticated women, sex objects or female body parts, now there is a stereotype of a different kind. She is the airbrushed, sexually aggressive babe.

From every surface, these commercial messages tap into our anxieties, expose and create vulnerabilities and tell us grown women that we need to be younger, smoother and firmer.

Try spending a day looking at these messages through the eyes of a girl who is trying to form an idea of what it is to be female. By the time they're seventeen, girls have seen 250,000 TV commercials telling them they should be aspire to be a sex object or have a body size it is almost impossible to achieve. When I took a fresh look around me, it was no wonder that by the time my younger daughter Clio was five, she was asking: 'Why do people thinks boobs are so important?' Advertising works by making us feel we are missing something. If it still works on us as adult women, how much more powerful and damaging is it to youngsters looking to find their place in the world and who don't know any better?

As a teen in the eighties, before the explosion of expectations about how every female in the world should look, I had a scrapbook. When I found a picture of a model I liked, I would cut her out and put her in that scrapbook. It was a peculiar form of torture. I would spend hours trying to work out how these girls looked so perfect, when I saw none of these flawless beauties in the real world. I was still growing – my skin was in turmoil and my features were not yet in proportion. And to this day, 30 years later, I still remember the pain of feeling that I would never measure up to the girls with perfect skin and delicate noses. It was only many years later that I realised how much of those magazines were made up of a very small and select band of superhuman-looking girls, attended to by teams of stylists and make-up artists, and perfected by airbrushes.

So, imagine how our daughters feel now, with those images multiplied a thousand times over in magazines deliberately aimed at them – and with the implicit message from society that they too can look like celebrities if they invest the time and money, or are willing to go under the needle, the laser or the knife. As one girl in a GirlGuiding UK survey explained: 'When I was eleven, I read a teenage magazine for the first time and that is when it kind of clicked: "I should be like this."'

The effort involved in living up to these ideals takes up an extraordinary amount of time and mental energy. I have spoken to children who will spend an hour getting their hair 'just so' on Monday mornings so they look like the celebs they've seen on TV at the weekend – but who somehow don't have time to eat breakfast to set them up for a day at school.

But of course, it's not a fair comparison. Studies consistently find that the women on TV and in magazines are 15 per cent thinner than the average woman, and the advent of Photoshop means that 99 per cent of magazine pictures have now been digitally perfected. But somehow, even if they know that, girls can still take these images to heart.

WHAT YOU CAN DO

❋ **Limit your child's exposure to beauty and fashion magazines.** Most fashion magazines carry more ads for beauty products than they do articles. You may have learned how to filter these messages out, but young girls haven't. There are lots of other interesting publications you can leave around the house. If she's interested in fashion, by all means look at the latest editions, but read them together and talk about how impossible it would be to recreate these pictures in the real world. Don't make celebrity magazines your regular reading material, because they can lead impressionable girls to mimic the occupational self-obsession of celebrities.

❋ **Teach her how to look in the mirror.** It may sound absurd, but in today's hypercritical culture, we may have to train our girls to look at their reflections and to see the good. Tell her to question the filter she is using to look at herself. Show her how to go from head to toe, appreciating and accepting the loveliness of her body and the functions it can perform. Ask if she is looking at herself with her real eyes or her critical eyes.

❋ **Model a healthy self-image.** Comment on things you like about yourself that are deeper than skin, like how healthy or energetic you feel. Let your daughter hear you compliment yourself in specific ways.

SELFIES: SELF-EXPRESSION OR SELF-OBSESSION?

'I got a camera for my birthday when I was twelve, but it would never have crossed my mind to take dozens of pictures of myself. But now my daughter never stops taking pictures of herself to send to her friends. I'm worried she is not seeing the real world anymore with her own eyes. Everything has to be seen through a lens.'

CARLA, 45

'My ten-year-old daughter is constantly taking selfies, but it doesn't seem very realistic, or very healthy for that matter, to cast herself as the star in every scene.'

JULIETTE, 41

In the changing rooms at the pool, thirteen-year-old Anna tips back her head so her mane of long brown hair cascades down her back. Today she is dressed in a turquoise bikini, comprising three small triangles and some string. With an iPhone at the ready, she tries several poses in the full-length mirror to get the shot that best captures her body. As she reviews the shot, Anna likes what she sees. The pose is key in these pictures. By jutting her hip out just so and angling the camera above her head she can create the best impression of slimness and make her legs look longer. Anna's stomach is also washboard flat, not because she has yet had to diet but because her child's body has only just started turning into a woman's. And holding the phone high up also slims down her face and sculpts her cheekbones. Then there's the expression, which on this occasion is a picture of blasé insouciance, as if having a body like this was the most natural thing in the world, which so far it has been. For those finishing touches, Anna tries a variety of filters, choosing a softening effect that gives that all important airbrushed skin tone.

Now she is ready to upload to all her networks: Twitter, Facebook and Instagram.

It is on these networks that you see the stories of our daughters' girlhoods. They start out presenting themselves with pictures of fluffy pets and on school trips, and then decide that their real selves aren't quite enough – so they experiment with image manipulation, and in turn are manipulated by the response.

Last week Anna posted a shot of herself dressed in skiing gear that attracted four likes. But when she posts her bikini shot, the response explodes. Within a couple of hours 140 people have liked it and commented with remarks like: 'You are literally so hot', 'hawt' and 'hot damn' – all variations on the highest form of praise that young people can shower on each other.

Of course, if you met her Anna would come across as a normal pubescent girl. But each time she reveals a little more skin, her online approval rating goes up, and it's hard not to get hooked on creating this supermodel version of herself with the help of filters and airbrushing apps.

For others in her class, seeing Anna looking so good makes them reflect painfully on their own perceived short-comings. They include Eva, who replies with the single word 'Skinny' followed by lots of downturned smiley faces, because her natural body type means she can only aspire to Anna's long limbs.

However, emboldened by the positive response to Anna's bikini shot, her friend Omani gives it a try. But although her attempts are admired, they don't pull in quite the same number of likes, causing her to realise that her place on the beauty hierarchy in her class is lower than she might have hoped, and making her think she must try harder.

In a way, girls have always posed for pictures like these. What woman hasn't got a faintly embarrassing picture of herself getting ready for the school disco and pouting as she tries to find out what being 'sexy' looks like? But the fact we no longer have to take such shots to the chemist to be developed and the explosion of camera phones means selfies have become the new mirror. According to the Pew Research Center, 91 per cent of teenagers have posted a selfie.

In a world where girls think they have to be humble and put themselves down or they get called full of themselves, maybe the self-promoting selfie showing she is proud of her body or feels lovely, funny, fun or sexy is not always a bad thing. But the risk comes when selfies become a constant attempt to get the validation girls seek for their appearance but are not getting in the real world. It is for this reason that, left unchecked, social media platforms can start to run a girl's life as she ceaselessly monitors her popularity ratings in the form of 'likes'.

The reality is that selfies don't always represent ourselves. Artfully styled photos are an attempt to boost our stock. Girls may take dozens, but the ones they post are the idealised images, altered with filters and airbrushing apps, that they don't always find it easy to live up to.

Social media starts off turning girls into little PR agents for their own images and, like PR, it can be addictive to be able to manipulate the truth. The story of their lives starts being told through a series of carefully managed, airbrushed picture opportunities. And since the artfully posed 'duckface' and pout became par for the course, the bar has been raised much higher by bikini shots, as modelled by Kim Kardashian and Rihanna. While celebrities may need these images to prolong million dollar careers, while our girls are growing up, we have to ask if posting endless versions of themselves is the best use of their time.

Here 'likes' and mentions and tags get fiercely monitored and traded in time-consuming trades that steals hours of the day and a major part of a growing girl's headspace. And even though the craze was started by celebrities, the latest research shows that our daughters are in fact more influenced by the swimsuit shots of other girls their age than by those of celebrities.

Even when girls retouch their own images, their brains do not always compute that others are doing it too. They just think everyone is skinnier and more gorgeous than them.

A study has found that the self-esteem of girls who spend a lot of time on Facebook is likely to be damaged after seeing the endless parade of posed, perfected pictures of their friends. The more time they spend on the network, the more they compare their bodies to those of their peers and the worse they feel about their appearance.

To fight back, they try to present an image of perfectionism that becomes harder to live up to when there is no lens between them and the real world. For some girls who are insecure about their looks – and don't get the approval they crave – managing such images and trying to be more successful in the cyberworld than the real world can become a compulsion. This perfectionism can also make it hard to admit when things aren't as rosy as they appear in the pictures.

After moving beyond the fluffy pet picture stage, it is often younger girls who are experimenting with their sexuality who post the sexiest ones. Later, the need for more revealing posts will give way to less revealing images designed to show how fun their lives are and reinforce social hierarchies and friendship groups. A good measure of how a girl's self-worth is evolving is how long she still needs to keep posting the more scantily-clad 'admire me' shots.

The poignant thing, looking at these pages, is how soon girls start to get nostalgic for their not-so-long-ago childhoods. They are hardly out of the sexy selfie phase when they start posting old primary school line-ups, baby pictures and nursery school birthday parties. It's as if the pressure to look good so young is already making thirteen- and fourteen-year-olds reminisce about a simpler life.

WHAT YOU CAN DO

※ **Ask her what it is she is trying to say about herself.** Suggest that she considers, in a non-critical way, the image she is trying to project. On what basis does she want to be judged? Does she want to join an online beauty pageant in which anyone who feels like it can be the judge?

※ **Take selfies that are about personality, not just looks.** Help her make a collage of the things that represent her, like her hobbies and the things in her life that inspire her. Tell her it's these things that make her special, not how she appears to other people.

SELF-HARM

How to stop girls becoming their own worst enemies

'She did go on (self-harming) websites a lot, late into the night. She was talking to her peers; they were egging each other on. She was at a very academic school, and there was this little group who competed to see who had the most cuts and who could do it in the most extreme way.'

RACHEL, WHOSE DAUGHTER STARTED SELF-HARMING AT THE AGE OF FIFTEEN

'Cutting was a coping method for me. It allowed me to feel physical pain instead of the emotional, because the physical is easier to understand and explain to others. But even so, I think adults would rather not know.'

COLLEEN, SEVENTEEN

'Sarah does it when she gets very low, generally when she's eaten less. She thumps her hips, pinches herself until she bruises, scratches a particular area on her hand until it bleeds.'

HEATHER, WHO DISCOVERED HER DAUGHTER WAS SELF-HARMING AT FIFTEEN

Most of us knew someone at school who bit their nails until they bled or chewed their hair.

But now self-harm is taking a more serious form, with cutting becoming more common. Among groups of close-knit girls it can spread quickly, thanks in part to dedicated community websites that encourage it, and some young adult books that have chosen it as an 'in' theme. The result is that such behaviour can go through classes like wildfire, with some girls even forming competitive cliques called 'cutting clubs'.

It is a subject that fills parents with terror. But as the age of self-harm sinks lower each year and the number of cases rises sharply, it's essential not only to head it off before it happens, but also to make sure our girls find safer outlets for any stress they feel.

The reasons a young person self-harms are complex. There is rarely a single trigger or event. Instead, it is caused by an escalation of feelings of helplessness, hopelessness and low mood. Children hurt themselves to distract from feelings of tension, and generally girls do it to blot out mental anguish and to feel a sense of control over themselves and their bodies.

To dismiss it as a form of attention-seeking is wrong as many forms are completely invisible, says Rachel Welch of the support website selfharm.co.uk. She told me she has come across girls who keep sharp objects in their vaginas or who wear shoes that are too small so that every step is agony. Another form is deliberate promiscuity, in which a girl repeatedly allows her body to be used or abused.

Self-harm may also have particular attraction for girls who already feel marginalised in their social lives, and for whom such behaviour gives them a sense of belonging among other youngsters who do the same. If your daughter has made such friends, they will mean a lot to her because she feels understood by them.

If you discover your daughter is self-harming, or even just visiting the websites, tread softly at first. Even if you can see how unhealthy these sites are, abruptly forbidding her to access them can set her off in a panic that she will be losing face, and that in turn can trigger a serious episode of self-destructive behaviour. It's a challenge, but you will have to prove that you understand her better.

How to talk to children about self-harm when they are young

Because self-harm has a reputation for spreading extremely quickly through year groups, most parents are simply too petrified to even raise the topic for fear it will put the idea in their children's heads. But Rachel Welch says there are age-appropriate ways to talk to your daughter without being explicit about cutting or self-wounding.

First, talk to your children about emotions. The bottom line is that self-harm is much less likely to happen if a child is allowed to speak openly about her feelings, no matter how uncomfortable they are.

In young girls, find out what names for feelings your daughter already knows and help her to recognise and be open about others like resentment, worry, frustration and anger. Then talk about how you cope when you find yourself in the stressful situations we all face in our lives. Talk about the methods that have worked for you.

If you hear that a classmate in your daughter's class is self-harming, talk to your daughter about healthy and unhealthy ways of expressing anxiety. To make it less frightening, tell your child her classmate is not trying to kill him- or herself, but is more likely to be looking for a way to relieve their stress. Explain that it's better to relieve those feelings in a way that won't leave long-lasting scars, which she will never be able to get rid of, and that doesn't put her at physical risk so serious she may end up in hospital, as more than 12,000 young people did last year, according to NHS statistics.

Tell her that if she ever feels the need to harm herself because she cannot find the words or methods to relieve her anxiety any other way, she can always talk to you – and you will never be angry, no matter what she has to say.

WHAT YOU CAN DO

- **Don't panic.** Easier said than done, but remember that self-harm is rarely a practice for suicide. It's about regaining control, creating an outlet for emotions and wanting to be heard. Devote real time to your relationship. Tell your daughter you want to listen to her – and hear what she really has to say.

- **Be vigilant for signs.** Is your daughter becoming more secretive, spending more time alone, distancing herself from friends and family or wearing long sleeves? Teens who are self-harming often wear too many clothes in warm weather.

- **Filters.** It will be a lot harder for your daughter to get caught up in the darkest recesses of the self-reinforcing websites that actively encourage anorexia and self-harm if they are more difficult to access. Tell her there is peer pressure on the internet too – from people she has never met – and if people are in a bad place emotionally, sometimes all they want is to draw others into their pain.

CYBER SELF-HARM

Every day after getting home from school, the first thing Ellie would do was switch on her laptop. Then she browsed her Facebook page, checked for updates from friends she had seen just half an hour earlier and commented on the latest cute pictures of her baby niece.

But that wasn't the only social networking she did. Later, during a break in her homework, she would curl up on the bed and log on to Ask FM, a social network where young people pose questions and invite anonymous answers. There, under her profile name, she would ask a question such as: 'What is the best thing about me?'

But Ellie didn't have to wait for a response from her friends, or any of the millions of strangers on the network. Instead, she logged back in under the name of another user she had created, an alter ego called 'Staceeey'. Then she scrolled to her question and answered it herself: 'Nothing. You are no one.' Over the course of a year, while her parents assumed Ellie was studying for her forthcoming exams, the teenager was posting dozens of vicious remarks about herself.

Ellie says: 'I knew it was me writing that stuff, but on screen it wasn't me. My own posts would say I was ugly, I was useless, I wasn't loved ... all the stuff going round in my head. If I saw it in black and white coming from "other people", it helped get it out there and make it real.'

'My friends were trying to stick up for me against these mysterious trolls, so to keep up I had to post insulting messages about them, too, calling them slags. It was killing me to see them get so angry on my behalf, and I knew I had to stop.

But it was never about hurting people. It was about hurting myself.'

Ellie may never have cut herself. But the teenager was engaging in another form of self-harm, one which used words instead of razor blades. She was lucky. When another mother asked her mum, Sue, how she was coping with her daughter being cyber-bullied, Sue begged Ellie to tell her what had been going on. She was shocked that her daughter had seemingly kept the hurtful abuse to herself. Yet Ellie has still never admitted to her mother that she posted the comments herself. To this day her parents think she was a victim of vicious trolling by strangers. Crippled by embarrassment, Ellie decided to confide in adults who run a self-harm help website. It seems that on closer investigation, a growing number of girls who say they are being bullied online are actually posting the abuse themselves. In fact, cyber self-harm, both public and anonymous, appears to be much more common than most of us could have guessed. In a recent study of more than 600 first-year university students, US researchers found that 9 per cent had posted toxic remarks about themselves. Twenty-three per cent of those who did this posted remarks once a month, 28 per cent once or twice a year.

An investigation into cyber-bullying cases by an online question-and-answer network, Form Spring, now renamed Spring Me, also hit an obstacle when it was found that many of the bullying attacks were by the 'victims' themselves. British police say they, too, are increasingly inclined to look at the bigger picture when asked to investigate claims by families that their children are being cyber-bullied.

The reasons for cyber self-harm are varied. Self-trolling can pre-empt criticism from others or externalise the self-loathing encouraged by an image-obsessed society. For teenagers with little experience of how to handle their feelings, bringing their pain out into the open can make it feel more real and important. Understandably, most young people are too ashamed, embarrassed and confused by their behaviour to admit what they have done.

But if your daughter claims she is being bullied online, it's worth being vigilant – and if you suspect she's posting these comments herself, don't confront or shame her. Above all, self-harm is an urgent and very real cry for intervention, however it's expressed. Even if the comments are fabricated, the feelings they express are completely real.

WHAT YOU CAN DO

❊ **Check their privacy settings.** One clue that a young person may be actively seeking out bullying is if they turn off their privacy settings to boost the chances of attracting vitriolic comments from strangers. Some cyber-watchdogs believe that as many as 80 to 90 per cent of children who say they are being cyber-bullied do not have the security options switched on – and that sometimes this is deliberate.

❊ **Review your relationship.** If it has got to the stage where your child needs to do this in order to seek help, she is trying to get someone to listen. Try the communication techniques in part two to rebuild your bond.

CONNECTED

Growing up with the internet

Thanks in part to being given smartphones to play with while they are still in their prams, kids are finding their way around the internet sooner than ever. Now that it's a part of everyday life, we should start by teaching kids about all the positives. After all, it is not the web itself that's the problem – it's an amazing tool – it's how some people use it that is the issue.

For children, the virtual world is just as real to them as their everyday life. In the same way, we parents need to help make it just as safe a space for them.

WHAT YOU CAN DO

- **Place your limits early – as soon as they are using technology.** If you give children unlimited access to the internet from the start, they regard it as a right that should be available to them around the clock, not a privilege, and that makes it harder for you to apply the boundaries that will protect them.

- **Give them rules.** Before they start surfing alone, introduce a safety promise in return for web usage. They may not stick to every rule, but at least you've set them off thinking about the issues. Rules can be things like:

  – If I see anything online that upsets me, I'll tell my parents.

  – If I'm not sure a website is OK, I will ask first.

- I won't give any personal information like my real name, address, age, phone number, school, passwords or what I look like to anyone online.

- I won't send pictures to anyone I do not know in real life, and I will not forward pictures of others.

- I will get my parents' permission before filling out forms for any competitions, surveys or services.

- I won't write or forward threatening, unkind emails, instant messages or postings on websites or blogs – even anonymously.

- I won't answer email or instant messages from someone I do not know.

- I won't arrange to meet anyone in person or online via webcam that I meet online without my parents' permission. I know that people may not be who they say they are online.

- I won't install software programs or file-sharing programs without permission.

- I won't divulge my passwords or use other people's passwords to access their accounts or buy things.

- I will stick to these rules whenever I'm at home, at a friend's house or on my phone. If I break them, I know I may lose the right to use technology.

OTHER WAYS TO KEEP CHILDREN SAFE

For younger children

❋ **Travel with them.** Younger kids are likely to be pleased and excited to have you surfing along with them to start with. Help them find a selection of sites they like, and make a list of favourites and tell them to stick to these if you are not with them. Most girls under the age of ten are happy just to use sites they already know.

※ **Keep control.** According to studies, youngsters are increasingly showing signs of compulsion in their use of tablets and smartphones, including taking their devices to bed and in some cases even preferring the company of gadgets to people. As many as four in ten teenagers believe they are addicted to the internet, with girls affected more than boys. As soon as your child starts using these devices, limit usage to half an hour and explain that any extra time is a privilege that has to be earned. Set a designated time every day for this – but make it only after homework is done.

※ **Don't let them use their device as an alarm clock.** If some youngsters had their way, their devices would be the last thing they look at when they go to sleep and the first thing they see in the morning. Unless you make it the rule that all phones are charged outside the bedroom, your child could easily be texting and on social networks well into the night, at a cost to their health, growth and academic progress.

※ **Give them safe search engines.** Google and Yahoo are amazing resources, but the access they give children is just too wide. Give them a list of kids' search engines like KidsClick and Ask Jeeves for Kids. They are fun, written in easy-to-read language and, best of all, no pornographic or sexual content will come up – even if they were to ask for it.

※ **Monitor YouTube.** Kids are increasingly using YouTube as an alternative to TV. It is also a great educational tool, but the recommended videos that appear on the right-hand side of the screen can quickly branch off into unpleasant territory. Switch on the safety mode in the bottom of the screen. It takes just minutes.

❊ **Don't let your child keep a computer in their room.** Whereas once families had one large main computer, many households now have to up to eight different internet-enabled mobile devices. Don't allow kids with gadgets to disappear into their bedrooms for hours on end. Make sure the iPad is used in the general living area and returned to the same spot every time. It's not failsafe, but your child will be less tempted to wander off into the darker corners of the internet if they know you could appear at their shoulder at any moment.

❊ **Teach scepticism.** Children are naïve; they start off taking everything they read on the internet at face value because they think it's written by grown-ups. But then it's hardly surprising they believe this when so many schools recommend using internet research for homework. Teach children that information on the web is not always reliable. Ask them to work out who created the site and what it's for. For example, does it have a logo, or does it say what the sources of the information are? Can they tell if it's based on opinion or fact?

❊ **All that glitters is not gold.** Tell children not to be lured by offers of free prizes or to click on banners that claim they've won things. Tell them that ads and pop-ups are never as good as they look and never to fill in forms or enter competitions without permission.

OTHER WAYS TO KEEP CHILDREN SAFE

For older children

❊ **Switch it off.** From early on, turn off your home's broadband connection at a set time every night. Start as soon as your children are surfing on their own – and make it non-negotiable. Apart from heading off the temptation to wander into unsuitable sites, late night internet use is one of the factors that can lead to perpetually exhausted, bad-tempered children. Make sure your child's smartphone is charged overnight in the kitchen so you know she is not using it under the covers.

❊ **Make it a two-way conversation.** Nagging your daughter by constantly saying, 'You're on the computer too much' or waiting to catch her on unsuitable websites to tell her off isn't constructive. In the same way that you asked her what she did at school that day, ask her which sites she visited – and make it clear you are going to stay interested. Praise her when she shows self-control with her screen time and model it yourself.

CYBER-BULLYING

'You see it happening to other people first. Sarcastic comments next to photos like, "I love what you're wearing" or "You're so pretty". It's often about young people working out their place in the school hierarchy or trying to see how much power they have. Most of the time you're a bystander and you don't say anything because you don't want it happening to you.'

ALYSSIA, FIFTEEN

'When I started to be excluded by my friends at school, it quickly spilled onto the internet. I would have liked to have come home from school and not have worried about it, but it follows you wherever you go. First you start seeing other people getting the invites to the parties on Facebook – and the pictures of the events you didn't go to. Then you see general comments about the type of outfit you've been wearing. You're pretty sure it's a reference to what you've been wearing that day, but you can't say anything. It creates massive insecurity.'

ALEXIS, FOURTEEN

Warn your daughter that, unfortunately, in this day and age, it's quite likely someone will post something unpleasant or untrue about her on the internet. It's important to talk to her about cyber-bullying before it crops up – otherwise by the time it happens she will be too distraught to listen.

Talking to young people, there are some positive signs that, because they grow up seeing cruel remarks as a fact of life, they are becoming more resilient. The other good news is that young people overwhelmingly see the internet as a force for good in their lives, despite the dark corners that remain there. But this toughness can be hard-won, and, as parents, we cannot afford to underestimate the painful ripple effects of a cutting remark that hits on a girl's deepest insecurities.

ENGAGED

How to help your daughter use mobile phones safely

'Sometimes my friends and I message each other in lessons and the teacher doesn't even realise, even though they've installed mirrors at the back of the classroom. We're so good at it we can send messages under the desk and still look the teacher straight in the eye.'

JEMIMA, TWELVE

'One good thing about having my own phone is that I can keep in touch with my dad who lives 200 miles away. I send him messages and random thoughts that pop into my head, without asking my mum. I'd never use my phone to ring Dad though. In fact, I hardly use my phone to speak to anyone. I'd run out of things to say. It's much easier to text.'

SOPHIE, TEN

'The single most important possession in my life is my mobile. I use it for everything, and I'd be totally lost without it. I keep everyone up-to-date on Twitter, and I can use the internet to see what's going on in the world. I also use it as my diary and my radio. It's my whole world.'

SAMANTHA, THIRTEEN

'The odd thing is that we parents give kids phones for our own
peace of mind. But calling to tell me where she is is the last thing
Chloe uses her phone for. She may call me a couple of times a
week, but she probably sends about 150 texts to her friends.'

MAGDA, 39

Remember the days when you had to ask your parents for permission to use the big clunky household phone? Not only was the clock ticking on how long you talked for, it was also probably slap bang in the middle of the hall where the whole family could listen to every word. And of course, all you could do back then was speak and be spoken to, unlike today's gadgets which are TV, internet, cameras and everything else, rolled into one tiny, mobile package.

There is no denying how much easier mobiles have made our lives, and girls tend to want them as soon as possible as a way to gain more independence and to make their social lives more sophisticated, especially as phones are the most visible peer group possession of all. Even though they have grown up safely without them, by the time girls are at secondary school, most parents have bought mobile phones for their daughters because of the perceived dangers of allowing their girls to be out in the wide world alone.

All of this means that mobile phones occupy a difficult place in modern parenthood. Of all the technology that surrounds our children, they are the most difficult moving targets for parents to keep tabs on. Because they are by their very nature 'mobile' and 'personal', it's easier for girls to evade monitoring if they want to. From the outset it often seems to parents that once the phone is handed over the kids get most of the benefits. So, for your own peace of mind, lay some ground rules for yourself as much as your daughter. Remind her that you bought her the phone so you can keep in touch and to allow her a bit more freedom. Tell her that if she does not keep it charged up or never answers calls or texts, she will only increase your worry and she is not keeping up her side of the bargain.

WHAT YOU CAN DO

For younger girls

- **Don't use mobiles as pacifiers.** Now that there are a multitude of applications and video games on our mobiles, many parents use phones like dummies for kids to keep them quiet. Try not to go down this road. Children who regularly play games like 'Angry Birds' or 'Fruit Ninja' have been found to have lower scores in speech tests for both understanding language and speaking. Time spent on these gadgets also comes at a price. In one study it was found that while 21 per cent of four- and five-year-olds can find their way around a smartphone, only 14 per cent can tie their shoelaces.

- **Switch on the filters before you hand it over.** These days it's very easy to download adult content on most phones. Yet nine out of ten parents have failed to switch on the inbuilt safety measures on their children's phones.

- **Make her first phone a family phone.** For as long as possible, give her a family mobile phone that is for everyone in the family to use so she practises borrowing it and proves she can use it responsibly.

✄ **Check your phone usage around your kids.** If you constantly have your mobile glued to your ear when you are with your children or are texting at the supper table instead of finding out how their day has gone, what message are you sending? Few emails or texts are that important. Ask yourself if the reply or the call can't be made after their bedtime.

WHAT YOU CAN DO

For older kids

✄ **Buy an older model.** To start with, buy the previous model of the latest device because they are cheaper, and offer your daughter an upgrade as a reward for responsible use.

✄ **Set a password.** Setting a password is the first line of defence against thieves or other kids who may 'borrow' your child's phone to play practical jokes. Make it clear you expect her to let you know the password if you ask.

✄ **Set up a contact list.** Most parents give kids phones to keep them safe. So start by putting in the numbers for parents, grandparents, their school and emergency contacts.

✄ **Set boundaries.** Many mums now find it cheaper and easier to add their child's phone to their existing mobile bills, rather than trying to limit kids' usage with pay-as-you-go plans. Make it clear that unless they have bought and paid the bills with their own money, the phone is still yours and you expect it to be used responsibly.

✄ **Ban phones overnight from bedrooms.** Tell your daughter she must hand over her phone every night for you to recharge so she is not texting and accessing social networks under the duvet and losing out on sleep. This will also leave her sufficiently paranoid that you are keeping an eye on whether she is using her phone responsibly.

TEXTING

Teach her the language of texting. Because texting seems like a form of disembodied communication, teach your daughter that her words may be seen out of context – and therefore be read as nastier than she meant them to be. Tell her only to send the sort of texts she would like to get. Warn that what might seem like an in-joke – like calling her girlfriend a slut by text – can be taken extremely seriously by a friend's parent if they see it and can cause all sorts of ructions. Discuss how the speed and immediacy of texting might tempt her to make inappropriate comments before she's thought through the consequences.

Draw up the rules together upfront. Put together a brief contract to concentrate your minds. Explain upfront that the rules are there for her safety. Agree between you that if she doesn't abide by them then she may lose phone privileges. Unless your daughter is cyber-bullying, don't confiscate it completely as a phone is a teen's life. But do consider reducing talk plans or cutting off features.

Make her phone use her responsibility. If her usage is getting out of control, make your child responsible for her own phone by switching to pay-as-you-go and asking her to pay out of her own pocket money. However, many children will play up to this and use lack of credit as an excuse to be unavailable. Head teacher Charlie Taylor recommends making a rule where teens are not allowed to leave the house without a topped-up phone.

Ban texting during homework, meals and conversations. Make it clear to your daughter that eye-to-eye interaction and conversation have priority over phone messages. Explain that it's not enough for her just to be in the room.

SEXTING

'I have a friend who really liked this guy and he asked her to send him naked pictures. She begged him not to forward them to anyone. But of course they were all around the year within five minutes. She was really cut up and traumatised that everyone she knew had seen intimate parts of her. No one gave him a hard time for doing it – he was just being 'a lad' – and he acted like nothing had happened.'

MILLY, SIXTEEN

'For this generation, it feels like it's all happening in the wrong order. People my age should be asking each other for dates and getting to know each other first before swapping sexy pictures.'

FLO, SIXTEEN

'As soon as I arrived at school, I knew most people had seen the picture I had sent to the boy I liked the night before because they were staring and laughing. When my back was turned, I heard the words "slag" and "slut". But I did it because it's just normal. If a boy likes a girl,

the first thing he does is ask for your picture. But not
everyone gets theirs sent around the entire year group.'
SOPHIE, FOURTEEN

'I got a call from the head of the lower school who told me
the boys had been passing round a nude picture on their
phones in afternoon registration. My first instinct was: "You
must have the wrong child." I couldn't imagine my daughter
would ever have the confidence to pose nude. But when I
spoke to her, she didn't seem particularly embarrassed by
the picture itself. It was more the fact the girls in her school
were now being horrible because of the attention she was
getting. She even admitted that sending flirty messages and
pictures made girls more popular and the prettier ones
tended to get the most requests. I couldn't believe it.'
CHANDRA, 40

As she sat down to her homework in her bedroom, thirteen-
year-old Sophie heard the familiar chime of her mobile
phone. Among the usual messages from friends, there was
yet another text from a thirteen-year-old boy in her class. It
was the tenth from him that day, each one making the same
request: 'Sophie, send me a topless picture. You know you
want to. All I want is to see you naked.'

Such requests were not unusual for Sophie. So far, she
had always ignored them, or said a very firm 'no'. But like
many girls whose confidence is battered by the images
around them, she found this boy's persistence flattering. At
the back of her mind she also knew it tended to be the more
attractive girls at school who were asked by boys to send
them 'special' pictures. So Sophie peeled off her top, sat on

her bed and pointed the phone at her chest. She quickly followed it up with a text urging the boy not to pass it on. Too late. Within minutes, the picture was circulated to the rest of the boys in her class.

When Sophie told me her story, it seemed pretty typical of a practice that has become a way of life for our children. An NSPCC study revealed that 40 per cent of young people had taken part in sexting. For more and more children, such communication has simply become a way of life. Even so, it's too soon for us to allow our children to swap naked images with no boundaries at all.

Kids live online, so it's not surprising that they flirt online too. In a world where they often don't feel pretty enough, many girls are looking for a fix – an admirer to tell them how beautiful they are. Indeed it's swung so far that girls who don't get requests for sexts assume it's because they are unattractive. To boys, who are used to seeing thousands of porn clips, these images are casually traded like cigarette cards. Boys I spoke to didn't hesitate for a second to share them. Getting a decent selection of sexy images of the most attractive girls is a tangible, visual symbol of his powers of persuasion, his sway with girls. In a culture where the word 'gay' is still used as an insult, boys gather them to prove they are straight and feel like the macho stars they see in porn.

Yet though girls may think this is just part of the mating ritual, sexting can still have hugely disruptive effects on their school life, peer relationships and sense of trust in the world.

And even if girls want to be asked, the boys are still engaging in predatory behaviour. Girls may believe they hold all the cards, but the reality is the boys have the power.

Once, sexting was mainly the preserve of older teens. But the NSPCC study found that a third of under-eighteens have been affected by sexting and that girls as young as eleven are frequently asked to send intimate photos to boys they know – especially now that most children entering secondary school are given phones that double as cameras. And, inevitably, the requests girls get for pictures are swiftly followed by messages asking for oral sex. In short, sexting opens the doorway for boys to start treating girls like the actresses they see in porn videos.

For Sophie, that lesson has come too late. She has grown up in a world where boys have little respect for girls and where girls have little respect for themselves. Perhaps because Sophie has never known a time when trading images of body parts has not been part of courtship, she doesn't believe boys will ever stop. She says: 'Boys think they have the right to do this. They treat girls like dirt. It's just the way life is. Adults can't change that. I felt like a child when this happened. By sending those pictures, I've lost part of my childhood I can never get back.'

WHAT YOU CAN DO

❋ **Talk to them before it happens.** Children are curious about sex earlier than we think, so have the conversation early. As soon as they get their first phone, explain they should never send or forward pictures that would make other children uncomfortable, sexual or otherwise.

* **Explain the power dynamic.** Spell it out before it happens that as much as your daughter might like to believe a sext is an intimate message between her and a boy who likes her, the truth is that he will find it very hard not to treat a picture as a trophy to show off to his mates. Once it leaves her hands, she has no control over where it will end up.

* **Support, don't blame.** As a parent you are likely to be so shocked that your daughter has been sexting that your first reaction will be to confiscate the phone and ask her what she was thinking. After all, it's embarrassing for you too, and you will be worried about what other parents think. But as one mother told me: 'My daughter had already lost a lot of friends, and by taking away her phone I was making life even more difficult for her.' Your daughter is already likely to be upset and angry with herself. Instead, tell her you understand she made a mistake – and that can happen to anyone – and say you will do all you can to help her move on.

* **Give her tactics to respond.** Show how to respond to curiosity, teasing and lurid comments from classmates. Help her come up with a blanket response which is simply: 'I made a mistake. I have learned from it, and now I am moving on.'

* **Explain privacy.** Teens tend to have lost all sense of what is private and public. Explain that sexting is not private. If they want privacy tell them to use a diary.

* **Tell her about the consequences.** Children often struggle to get their heads round the implications of pressing a button or to see further into the future than next week. As one twelve-year-old said to me about some bitchy remarks she posted on Snapchat: 'I only sent them to my friend. Why would she pass

them on?' Tell her that knowing how technology works is not the same as knowing how people work, that best friends and boyfriends can change fast and that pictures in the wrong hands can be impossible to erase and may come back to haunt her when she is older.

- **Give her a mental checklist before sending any picture.** Children love exchanging pictures, so it's not realistic to ban them. But get her to ask herself a set of questions before she presses the send button – and to recognise and listen to the voice in her head that says: 'Maybe this isn't a good idea.' For younger girls those questions should be things like: 'Would I be happy with everyone in my class seeing this?' For older girls tempted to send pictures, ask if she'd like the recipient's mates to get a look too.

FRIENDSHIPS
Best friends or worst enemies

'I have just started secondary school and I am not sure
what "popular" means anymore. I used to think it meant
you are a person that lots of people like because you are
a nice person. But at my new school it seems to mean that
your parents are rich, and that you are pretty and thin.'

VANESSA, ELEVEN

'If I went up to the popular group at school, they'd giggle
and walk off. It's because I've got spots. It's really brutal.'

ANYA, TWELVE

'They all have labels for themselves according to what they look
like – there's the spotty ones, the geeky ones, the fat ones, the
pretty ones. It's much more defined than it was in my day.'

JOANNA, 39

'In my child's group at school, there's something called the
Ace Gang. They are the clique of the richest, prettiest girls
in the class. In other words, the self-styled "beautiful people".
They are all on the skinny side with straight hair and the most
stylish clothes – and they nearly all date older boys at the
nearby boys' school. I was absolutely horrified when I found
out this clique actually had a name, which seemed to imply
everyone else was inferior. I was even more shocked when I

spoke to a mum at another school in the area, who said there was also an Ace Gang in her child's class too. It's like these girls are trying to create a new class of super-perfect beings.'

ROSALIND, 44

'It seems like all the popular girls have to be pretty, and the girls who are not are side-lined. They seem to mention each other's looks before they mention anything else.'

JULIA, 39

When the Children's Society asked children what made their childhood happy, friendship was the factor they mentioned most often. For a girl, having friends who she can be herself with is probably the single most important factor in making her feel good about herself – and in wanting to go to school. Having a circle of playmates helps a child see she is likeable to the outside world. It builds her self-esteem because she knows friendship is a choice. Further into the future, the relationship lessons she learns in her tween years also help her choose healthy adult relationships.

From the other side of the school gates, it often feels like we have to leave our children to it. Yet even from the outside, we can still help even young children to identify healthy friendships that are supportive and helpful and which prepare them for the future.

WHAT YOU CAN DO

For younger girls

- **Organise play-dates.** There are some mums who don't make this a priority, often because a child is their second or third, or because they just don't have the time or inclination. Yet the more your daughter is able to role play and play pretend games, the more she will be able to decode the emotions of others and read them. You will also be able to develop friend-ships with other mothers whose values about child-rearing chime with yours.

❊ **Don't be a helicopter parent.** In the early days, play-dates are also the cement that builds friendships. But don't hover over your children and her playmates. Give them space to feel comfortable with each other. A study by psychologist John Gottman found that creative imaginative play is the core fea-ture of friendship – but that it quickly stops once parents burst the play bubble.

❊ **Try to see life from your daughter's point of view.** Remember how important your friendships were at school. Do you recall how it felt when one of your friends inexplicably stopped talking to you? Or the mortification you felt when you had no one to play with at break? Remember her friendships will feel like life or death to her. Of course, as an adult you can see the big picture: that you survived. You will also have learned that friendships come and go. But at the moment, your daughter is very much stuck in the school microcosm, which can be a claustrophobic place. Take all her concerns seriously.

❊ **Tell her not to take differences of opinion personally.** Your daughter can come home in tears simply because another girl said they didn't like her favourite pop star. Really these sorts of remarks are attempts by other girls to work out who's allowed in their group and who isn't, which is why differ-ences of opinion get taken so seriously. Even so, you will be encouraging your daughter to be an individual if you tell her everyone is entitled to her own views.

- **Tell her never to expect to have just one perfect best friend.** Explain that no one person can meet all her needs and that she should build a circle of friends with lots of different people in it, each with something different to offer.
- **Explain that friendship problems are inevitable.** Don't pretend that everything will be rosy in the playground. Explain before they happen that bust-ups are an inevitable part of life – and friendships don't always last forever. Talk about fall-outs you've had with your friends, what caused them and how they turned out. Sometimes people grow apart, and there's no reason they can't move their friendship to a less intense phase.
- **Don't wait until it's too late.** If you wait until your child is already excluded, left out or bullied after a playground row, it's too late. She's already too upset to listen to your advice to stand up for herself. Instead of allowing her to cast herself as the victim, teach her upfront how to be assertive without being aggressive. Get her to role play dealing with difficult playground scenarios, like a friend who won't let her play with another friend. It may not come naturally to her, but at least you are giving her the tools to handle these situations positively.
- **Teach her that everyone has feelings.** If you build empathy in your child, she will learn this skill too and is less like to bully others. Tell your children to be friendly and polite to peers whether they are friends or not, because everyone has feelings.

✼ **Teach her that questions can be the best defence.** Teach your child to have the confidence to question why another girl is saying hurtful things. It has the same effect as pouring salt on a slug. Teach her to simply say, 'Why are you saying that?' or, 'What's your point?' Many girls will simply back off when asked to account for their remarks.

✼ **Get older kids to help.** One of the most underused resources we have are older siblings, cousins or friends who have recently navigated the stormy waters of peer group relation-ships and can act as mentors. Just talking to them about their recent experiences in the school environment helps younger children realise they're not alone.

✼ **Look at your own behaviour.** As one teacher told me: 'Nasty mums often have the nastiest children.' Ask yourself if you are bitching and gossiping at the school gate. If your child hears you judging and undermining, she will quickly learn to do the same, even if you think it's going over her head. Think twice too about reading gossip magazines, and turn off bitchy TV programmes.

✼ **Explain that being nasty will ultimately make her feel bad about herself.** Studies have found that people who bitch and gossip suffer lower self-esteem afterwards, while those who are kind and generous to others feel better about themselves. Remind her that unkind remarks say more about the person making them than they do about the victim.

✼ **Show you can't change other people, only the way you react.** Children who are mean are usually girls who need to temporarily shore up their fragile self-worth. Tell your daugh-ter the meanness says more about them than her.

✂ **Don't use the silent treatment.** Children who use the silent treatment, threaten not to be friends with other children and give others the cold shoulder most likely picked up the behaviour from their parents, according to a study by Brigham Young University. Researchers found that parents who attempt to control their children by ignoring them teach them to treat their peers in the same way. Be a role model even in the subtle way you treat others.

WHAT YOU CAN DO

For older girls

✂ **Arm her with coping strategies.** To stay looking 'cool' in front of the clique, your daughter might find it hard to get out of situations she's not happy with. She may not want to take drugs or alcohol, but may find herself swept up in the moment and not know how to get out of it. Give her the tools to escape so she can still save face, like shifting the responsibility for the decision to you.

✂ **Ask her to listen to her values.** Ask your daughter to recognise when something she is asked to do by her friends conflicts with what she feels is right. Tell her never to respond to a 'dare', which is inevitably someone else trying to persuade her to do something dangerous they would get into trouble for. Explain that being a true friend is about wanting the best for someone.

✂ **Teach her to practice saying no.** Tell her that always saying yes doesn't make people like her more or make her a better friend. Explain that not wanting to go against the grain or cause a fuss might lead to her doing things she isn't comfortable with. Tell her she will get more respect from her peers if she trusts her own judgement.

BULLYING

'These days, people my age are more interested in Twitter than Facebook because you can flick through it really quickly, particularly in lessons. Unfortunately, the move over to Twitter means bullying has followed too. On one occasion, a girl in my lesson tweeted: "I hate it when I have to sit next to people I can't stand." The girl next to her read it on her feed and was really upset.'

SOPHIE, FIFTEEN

'When I was about thirteen, a group of boys at my school started bullying me on Facebook. There was no reason. They just seemed to hate me. It wasn't to my face. Instead they'd refer to me in the third person as a "him". They'd comment on photographs posted by my friends and suggest things like: "Why doesn't 'he' – meaning me – try out for the football team?" I didn't tell the school because I didn't think they'd do anything about it. In fact, I didn't tell even tell my mum. I was too embarrassed to admit what was happening.'

CHARLIE, SIXTEEN

'Overall I'd say technology makes my life better because I use it for so many things, like listening to music and finding out new stuff. I have learned a lot about science from YouTube videos and seen inspiring lectures on the TED website. But looking back, I'd also say the horrible things people say to each other on the internet has made me lose my innocence earlier. I've lost my faith in human nature sooner than I would have liked to.'

LUCY, SEVENTEEN

No matter how many anti-bullying policies are in place in schools, there will be times when your daughter will face cruel remarks from other girls – or indeed may be the source of them.

Very few girls escape completely. Nasty remarks which were once made in the heat of the moment and then forgotten about are now set in stone on Facebook or in text messages, where they can fester, drag in others and sometimes turn into full-scale classroom feuds.

Girls' developing judgement can also falter because they can make remarks hidden behind the safety of a computer screen. Messages can get misinterpreted and rumours spread. Exclusion from parties and sleepovers becomes all too obvious when pictures of the event get posted on the internet. As one parent told me: 'They just don't think what they are doing.'

Feuds can sometimes can go on for weeks without parents having an inkling. Too often, girls say nothing because they are terrified you will wade in there in their defence – and make everything much worse. Your daughter may also panic because she's the one who has to face the other girls day in, day out, not you. She will also dread you taking away her phone or computer, which are her lifelines. Her ideal solution is for the problem to magically disappear.

In this fraught and combustible environment, it's imperative that parents warn girls long *before* it happens. If you leave it until your daughter is in tears because her friend has called her 'a fat slag', by then she will be too hurt for anything you say to get through to her. Even before you need to, tell her that cruelty and meanness is often due to insensitivity, insecurity, lapses of judgement and aspects of human behaviour she can't control – that she's not always to blame, and she shouldn't be cruel either

Tell her that bullying is more than just obviously cruel words; it is also ignoring people, leaving them out, pulling faces and using a sarcastic tone of voice. It doesn't matter how 'annoying' she or others judge another child to be, it's never justified. If she ever catches herself thinking that another person somehow 'deserves' the treatment they are getting, ask her to question that thinking.

WHAT YOU CAN DO

- **Don't assume your daughter is an angel.** Almost all the mothers I spoke to whose girls were involved in cyber-scraps said it was never their daughter's fault. But of course they would think that, because they've only heard their child's side of the story – and the one designed to portray them in the best light. Acknowledge that it's going to be hard to get to the bottom of who said what to whom. Tell her you won't be angry if she tells you the whole truth and that you'd prefer to be fully in the picture so you are in the best position to help.

- **Ask your daughter to record what's been said.** If your daughter is seriously under attack from a cyber-bully, it will help her feel more empowered to print off or write down the times and dates of the comments. It will also make her think twice about sending messages that will inflame the situation. If needs be, the school will take the issue more seriously if it goes to that level.

✦ **Help her stand up for herself.** If your daughter makes it clear she's not going to be pushed around, bullies quickly move on. They can even go on to be amicable if they realise your daughter is a force to be reckoned with.

✦ **Help her to get through it.** If you find your daughter is being cyber-bullied, don't go in all guns blazing to confront the other girl, her parents or the school. This is what children fear most – that you will make the whole situation worse. Work out with her how she wants to approach the situation. Telling her that to ignore it won't work, as the chances are she has already been trying to ignore it for some time. Give her the skills she needs to deal with the people who are bullying her. Tell her to explain to the bully what behaviour she wants her to stop – and show her how to state clearly that even though they may never be friends, that does not give the other girl the right to be mean about her.

✦ **Tell her about trolling.** Even the most successful and beautiful people in the world get trolled. If it ever happens to your daughter, make it clear that these remarks are not based in reality. They are spawned from the insecure depths of the people who post them.

✦ **Play down anonymous comments.** Teach girls that the comments from people who won't put their names to a comment should count for nothing. Explain that, freed from accountability, human beings may feel liberated to say the first thing that comes into their heads, whether these comments are true or not. All too often, they are provocative remarks simply designed as bait to elicit a response.

THE POWER OF THE CLIQUE

Up until the age of around seven, friendships are relatively simple and uncomplicated. Girls often play in fluid and loosely formed groups of five or six, with maybe a best friend within that. Then around Year Four, girls tend to start to want to pick and choose, and more clearly defined friendship groups start to form.

The first lines may start to be drawn when a girl no longer wants to invite her whole class to her birthday parties and starts to select preferred friends for sleepovers. But, of course, our best friends can also be our worst enemies. Inevitably, one day your daughter will come home distraught that a friend refused to let her sit with her at lunch, didn't let her have the role she wanted in a game, or even said her name in the wrong tone of voice.

As she grows, much of this interaction will become so subtle as to be imperceptible to the adult eye. But fears that others are whispering about her – or her perception that others are sighing, tutting or raising their eyes around her – can send a girl's world crashing down around her ears. And while negotiating these stormy seas is a normal part of growing up, it doesn't make it easier for you – or her – to deal with. So start preparing her early.

As girls get older, the walls of these friendship groups get higher, like fortresses designed to exclude anyone else. By the time your daughter is about twelve, if not earlier, friends will be the main influence on how she talks, what she likes, how she dresses and her ideas about how she fits in.

Yet, though we all had friendship groups growing up, the lines now seem much more rigid. More than ever, British schools are becoming more like their American counterparts, with clearly defined popular cliques at the top of the pile. While boys will form themselves into friendship groups according to sports, musical taste or hobbies, girls tend to define themselves by a mixture of wealth, looks, likes, fashion, beauty or precociousness.

The need to be popular and be viewed as being in the 'in crowd' has become so pressing that the dominant popular groups now give themselves names, like Ace Gang or A-listers, to confirm their social dominance. As one mother told me: 'Anyone on the outside [of the group], like my daughter, already feels like a failure. Individually they are all nice enough girls. One of them talks to my daughter outside school, but she wouldn't be seen dead talking to her inside school.'

Yet even within the security of the clique, there is insecurity. As Rosalind Wiseman points out in *Queen Bees and Wannabees*, the trading of secrets, jealousy and competition means every girl feels she has to watch her back. Power plays within the group are likely to be such that she has to fight to stay a member by wearing the right clothes and saying the right things.

It doesn't help that, among girls who have been exposed to reality TV, there is a tendency for bitchy, excluding and judgemental behaviour to flare up even sooner. On programmes like *The Apprentice* and *Big Brother*, real people are regularly seen standing in judgement of others, back-stabbing behind the scenes, scheming and plotting. Girls have become increasingly critical of each other because they feel so vulnerable and judged.

The worry for parents is that peer pressure is also one of the key deciders of how soon your daughter decides to have sex and whether she drinks or takes drugs. The risk is that if she gets too deeply immersed in trying to impress others in her circle, a girl may lose her individuality, rather than being true to herself. The frustration for adults is that, as girls get older, they always seem to listen to their best friends – no matter how damaging their influence.

As Rosalind Wiseman points out: 'No matter what they do to her, she still feels her friends know her best and want what is best for her.' But even if she seems no longer to care about what you have to say, state your case anyway. She won't want to admit it, but what you think is still important. Even if she defends her friends to the hilt, there will have been moments when she will have been put in an uncomfortable position and encouraged to act against her values. So, deep down she will know perfectly well what you are talking about. Your message still has the chance of getting through, even if it's met by eye-rolling or denial.

In the best case scenario, she will avoid exclusive cliques altogether and choose her friends on the basis of who they are, not on their image. Indeed in a typical group of school children, 35 per cent belong to a 'popular group', 45 per cent are in the average group (not popular but have a handful of close friends) and 10 per cent have few or no friends, according to studies by social scientists. The safest place for your daughter is charting the middle way.

WHAT YOU CAN DO

※ **Reclaim the word 'popularity'.** Explain that true popularity means liking herself and having friends who like her for who she is. Explain the difference between good popularity, which is based on people liking her for who she is, and bad popularity, which is based on fashion, looks and status.

※ **Don't enable cliques.** In primary schools, when mothers often try to forge their children's friendships for them, sometimes class cliques get actively encouraged. Mums can tend to organise play-dates with other children based on whether the other child comes from a PLU family ('people like us'). By all means, gravitate towards parents with a similar approach to family life, but also check that you are not trying to engineer your child's relations based on more superficial values. Encourage your daughter to mix with a good range of boys and girls her own age.

※ **Talk to your daughter about the power of the clique.** Explain that people often seek out cliques because they feel insecure or crave the protection of the group. Talk to her about your experiences at school and how you fitted in – and stress that her individuality is always more important. Tell her how being in a clique can limit her and cut her off from other people who could be good friends. Don't let her think that because she is not in the popular group, she is not a valuable person. Remember that even girls who are at the top of the social tree don't always feel good about themselves, are often more feared than liked, and are anxious about how to maintain their position.

❊ **Don't encourage Queen Bee behaviour.** Mothers who were – or are – Queen Bees themselves secretly quite like seeing their girls being in the most exclusive cliques. If you are that mother, break the cycle because your daughter's individuality is worth more than that.

❊ **Talk about gossip.** Discuss with your child how easy it is to be carried away by the intrigue and drama of a new nugget of information. Ask her if she thinks it's really OK to pass on gossip about someone else, how she would feel if the gossip was about her, and what she is really gaining from it. Appreciate that girls often gossip to work out their place in the social order – and to gauge the reactions of both their friends and you to what other girls have done. Even so, tell her that while you can learn from others' behaviour, it's not acceptable to spread information about other girls maliciously.

❊ **Tell her that putting herself down won't make her more popular.** Some girls think that by putting themselves down they will seem less threatening and more likeable to their peers. At best, explain that it will make people feel sorry for her. At worst, they will dismiss or take advantage of her. It certainly won't win her more friends, because people like people who like themselves.

❊ **Give her outlets outside school.** Social circles inside schools can be fraught with power politics, so give her alternatives outside school so her classroom friendships are not the be-all and end-all. It means if she has a social hiccup at school, she still has the security of knowing there are people out there who know and like her with fewer strings attached.

✂ **Ask how her school is helping.** Many schools seem to accept cliques as an inevitable part of life. But these groups can poison the atmosphere and divide year groups into winners and losers. Ask what her school is doing to develop kids' healthy friendships. Do teachers seem aware of developing situations? Do they allow a certain group of outspoken alpha girls to dominate classroom discussions? Do they have a circle time or a discussion forum so that girls realise they are not alone with their friendship worries? Some schools also give children mentors in older classes and organise 'mix it up days' where pupils spend lunch sitting next to someone they don't know.

✂ **Explain that friendship is a matter of taste and timing.** Just because your daughter perceives she does not have as many friends as others doesn't make her an unlikable person. Friendship is also a question of meeting the right people at the right time – and just because she's not 'popular' now doesn't mean she won't have lots of good friends in the future.

HOW TO WORK OUT THE DIFFERENCE BETWEEN A GOOD AND A BAD FRIEND

Natalie Collins, who leads seminars about healthy relationships for young children aged seven and up, raises the following points to help them learn who's a good friend and who's not:

A bad friend is someone who:
Doesn't want me to play with other friends
Tells me that what I like is stupid
Laughs at me

Makes me feel sad

Pushes me to do things I don't want to

Thinks they are better than me

Hurts me

Says they will do something unkind to me if I do not do
what they want

Tells people my secrets

Tells me my friends don't like me

A good friend is someone who:

Plays with all my friends

Tells me I am good at doing stuff

Doesn't mind if I don't want to do stuff

I have lots of fun with

I don't have to play with all the time

Doesn't require me to like all the same things they do

Doesn't require me to do anything to stay being their friend

WIRED CHILDREN

Childhood and social networks

'The internet gives people too much power at an
early age. It reminds me of the book, *Lord of the
Flies*, where there aren't any rules and the cruelty
of young people quickly comes to the surface.'

CHARLIE, FIFTEEN

'My daughter had a really nasty falling out on Facebook with a
girl she had been best friends with since she was six. The reason
was really trivial, and it would have blown over if it hadn't then
been exaggerated out of all proportion when it was played out
for everyone to see on Facebook. All the other girls in the class
started getting involved. It turned into a show of bravado too as
the girls started calling each other "bitch" and "slut" for everyone
to see. She never told me while it was happening, although I
did notice that my daughter was withdrawn and preoccupied.
It was only when I asked why I hadn't seen the other girl
around that she admitted what was going on – and even then
I only got the full story from another mum in the class.'

JUDITH, 35

The last thing eleven-year-old Lucy does before she goes to
sleep, and the first thing she does when she wakes up in the
morning, is to reach for the smartphone she keeps next to her
bed. Even during the night, she never turns it off. Her biggest

compromise is putting it on silent. If it lights up during the night, she sometimes wakes up and checks her messages again in case she's missed anything. In the morning, her eyes are hardly able to focus before she checks all her social media platforms: Facebook, text messages and BBM, as well as the instant chat apps all her friends use like WhatsApp and Snapchat.

Lucy says: 'Sometimes overnight a big row has blown up. When that happens you just want to get the popcorn and a ring-side seat because most of them are so classic. Some people will start off by posting as their status updates – comments like "I hate so-and-so", and then it all kicks off. Most often it's other girls throwing insults and making each other look stupid. It can be vicious out there.'

By the age of nine, a quarter of children are on social networks. As our daughters grow, these become an integral part of their childhoods. With kids unable to spend as much time outdoors as they once did, social networks are also an important way of letting off steam and spending time with their mates. Children use them to do the same things we did when we were their age. They hang out together, make jokes, share gossip and flirt.

They also offer girls amazing opportunities to learn more about the world, and if used well, can become a key way for your daughter to find a voice to talk about the things that matter to her. But for all those pluses, from time to time, it does go wrong. Because they are public platforms, the impact of a mistake reaches further and faster than it would do if it were confined to a group of friends in the real world.

The internet also opens the door to people who will seek young girls out because they are impressionable, curious and feel so unconfident in today's hypercritical atmosphere that they want to hear flattery. Because youngsters don't know these people in the same way we knew the people in our social circle when we were younger, that also brings its own risks.

When talking about social networks, parents often fret about respecting their child's privacy. But, by its very nature, the internet is not a private place – it's a public space shared by millions of people, so the dangers are magnified. It would be as wrong to let your daughter wander through it without guidance as it would be to let her cross the road without telling her to look out for speeding cars.

By all means, use a light touch, keep a low profile and back off as much as possible until she has been on it a few years and has proved she knows how to handle herself. When I talk to girls of fifteen, I have often been impressed by how knowing they already are about the pitfalls – and how to handle them. But often that savvy has been hard-won by trial and error.

Never assume that just because you are not a young person living your life on these networks, you don't have anything to offer your daughter in learning how to navigate them. Although our girls may seem more familiar with the technology, they may not have yet learned to understand the motivations of the people that use it.

WHAT YOU CAN DO

✻ **Keep to the basic rules.** Keep the rules as simple as the green cross code so your child doesn't have to think twice. She should use privacy settings so that only the people she knows can see her. She should never send her photo to anyone she doesn't know. She should never say anything that she would not say to someone's face in the real world.

- **Stick to age restrictions.** Now that social network sites are evolving so fast, your girls might sign up to sites we barely even know about. Tell her to always ask your permission. Suggest she avoids anonymous question-and-answer sites because they give complete strangers power over her well-being that they have no right to.

- **Set a good example.** Model good behaviour by not being obsessively glued to your laptop and showing you can easily step away from it. Show self-control.

- **Visit the CEOP website.** Because, developmentally, they are still learning how the world works beyond their immediate lives, children often have a tough time understanding the sheer scale and potential dangers of social networks. They may also assume that as parents, we just don't want them to have fun and we are exaggerating the risks. The best teaching tools are safety videos which dramatise these issues in a way that kids can understand, like those found on the Child Exploitation and Online Protection Centre (CEOP) website.

- **Show how social media can be used for good.** One of the best uses of social media is the sharing of videos, images and articles about important issues. Make your own Facebook page an inspiring place which shows your commitment to different causes and ideas.

- **Teach her judgement.** Remind her that what she means to say may be read differently by other people on a social media page. If for one moment she hears a voice in her head asking, 'Is it really a good idea to post this?', tell her that's a clue that it's probably not.

❄ **Tell them who's watching.** Remind your girls that the internet is a public forum and the material they post can be seen by other parents, teachers or future employers. Once it has left their computer, pictures and comments can go anywhere.

❄ **Warn that they will get left out.** One of the most hurtful effects of social media is when girls see pictures of parties they were not invited to. It leaves girls feeling excluded, unpopular – yet unable to say anything. Warn them that this is likely to happen, that not everyone gets invited to everything. Ask them to be thoughtful when posting their own photos.

A WORD ON WEBCAM USE

Social networks can easily foster a growing girl's fantasy that she is in control of her sexuality, when she is not. When you are growing up in a world where you are constantly getting the message that it's important to be pretty, and someone pops up online to tell you you're gorgeous, it's hard not to have your head turned.

Webcams are a wonderful way for your daughter to keep in touch with friends and relatives. But they are also, quite simply, a door into your child's bedroom for anyone who can persuade her to open it, and it can get prised open with compliments intended to make a girl let down her guard.

According to the Child Exploitation and Online Protection Centre (CEOP), the sexier girls look in their profile pictures, the more likely they are to be targeted by adult predators. These predators no longer ask girls to send pictures, instead they will ask for live hook-ups. The latest figures show that the organisation received 6,291 reports of this, a rise of 880 on the previous year. More than 400 involved men asking girls to live up to the images they were projecting online by acting out sex acts. Another 1,500 were reports of perpetrators storing or spreading these images. At the thin edge of the wedge, in 513 cases, girls ended up meeting people they met online and being abused.

Jonathan Baggaley, Head of Education at CEOP, says: 'For many young people these days, their first sexual experience will be online. It's now very easy for a flirty conversation over a dating website to be turned into a webcam conversion that can lead them to being persuaded to do more and more online.'

'They can easily go on sites where they can randomly connect with strangers – sometimes six or seven at one time. Images of this kind of activity have also been found uploaded to child sex offender networks.'

The technology may have come a long way, but the lessons are still the same. Don't talk to strangers and don't invite anyone into your room who you don't know in real life.

TELEVISION
Switching off bullying

On *The Great British Bake Off*, a seventeen-year-old competitor is reduced to tears after being criticised by a judge for her 'soggy tart'. Behind the scenes of *The X Factor*, over on ITV, a contestant is bitterly complaining that her rival is being unfairly handed victory 'on a plate'. Still in the mood for more conflict? Then turn to *Big Brother*. Here a female housemate who has just entered the house is already in competition with the other women for the attention of the men on the programme.

So far, it's a typical nightly line-up of British television. Sitting in judgement of others and delivering our thumbs up or thumbs down verdict, as if it were a matter of life or death, has become a national pastime. Indeed, it's what passes for family entertainment. Every weekend, *The X Factor* alone regularly pulls in around 14 million viewers a night with its live shows – about half the total TV audience – and it's children who are among its biggest consumers. If you've ever seen children settle into the sofa for an evening of reality TV, you will know how utterly transfixed they are by the high drama, and how they also like to condemn. Monday mornings in the playground are spent sharing their judgements. Most of the viewers of shows like *Big Brother*, *I'm a Celebrity, Get Me Out of Here!* and *Britain's Next Top Model* are under the age of 24.

These shows create a world of throwaway friendships, rejection and exclusion which encourages criticism and bullying, and where everyone is divided into winners or losers. Beauty and sex are portrayed as ways to win friends and manipulate people. At a critical time in our girls' lives, these shows also teach them this is how the adult world works. Incidents of eye-rolling, heavy sighing, criticism and drama queen style outbursts come thick and fast in these shows. In a study by Brigham Young University, *The Apprentice* topped the list with 85 acts of verbal aggression per hour.

Even among an adult audience, who should know better, researchers have found reality TV programmes are the most likely of any format to influence behaviour. But, while adults have the life experience to see through the hype, children, who don't know any better, believe that what they see on TV is normal.

So, what lessons are we teaching our children when they see an average of 319 incidents of relational aggression on our television screens every week? How will they relate to their friends when the girls they aspire to be like on TV all bitch about each other behind their backs? Unless we help our daughters question these messages, they become professional mini critics.

Teenager Nicola Evans knows all too well how judgement-based programmes really do become reality. Every morning for months, when Nicola arrived at school, a clique of fifteen-year-old girls would follow her into the building, whispering remarks like, 'Morning, Ugly Betty', after the show of the same name.

Nicola told me: 'It was a four-minute walk, and I would have to brace myself for it. All they saw in me was someone a little bit overweight with glasses. They'd seen so many of these programmes, these girls saw nothing wrong with passing judgement on the way I looked in front of the whole school.'

'You either fitted into the so-called beautiful group of girls who wore loads of make-up, who were known as the Plastics and Barbies. Or you were in the also-rans who were called the Inbetweeners. Everyone else was labelled a loser.'

'The Barbies, in particular, would pride themselves on watching *Next Top Model*. The whole discussion at school the next day would be: "Do you think she's pretty?" "No, she's ugly. I wouldn't vote for her." It doesn't take much to start thinking like that about everyone around you.'

For Nicola, the hurtful remarks did not end when the credits rolled. 'Being told you aren't good enough in front of the whole schools hurts. When it really is happening to you, the memories don't go away when you turn the TV off.'

But should we really be surprised? Isn't this the inevitable consequence of a decade in which reality programmes have dominated our TV schedules? After all, there is strong evidence that children mimic behaviour they see onscreen. More than 1,000 studies have drawn a link between TV violence and aggressive behaviour in children. The difference is now that the shoot-outs and kung-fu kicks have been replaced with emotional violence, dressed up in designer clothes and set against glamorous backdrops.

Of course, cruelty in the playground has existed since the first little girl told a would-be playmate: 'No, you can't play with me.' But what has changed is how early our daughters witness adults behaving in this way – and how much it's presented as something to aspire to.

According to charity Kidscape, bullying is being seen in more young children than ever, even among the four- to six-year-old age group. It is also little girls, rather than little boys, who are more prone to copy verbal aggression on TV, according to a study by Indiana State University. While it used to be teenagers who cried themselves to sleep at night because they felt left out, didn't look 'right' or hadn't been invited to the right parties, teachers tell me they now see this phenomenon played out among primary school pupils.

WHAT YOU CAN DO

✂ **Be age appropriate.** Just because they're too old for CBeebies and it's before the watershed doesn't mean they're ready for everything else. Six-year-olds certainly shouldn't be parked alone in front of soaps. Make sure the programmes they are watching are appropriate for their age.

✂ **Watch TV with your child.** Parents can transform TV into a learning tool by watching with their children, rather than just leaving them to their own devices in front of a screen. Use what you see as a jumping off point for talking about difficult issues. Sit with them, question the judgements, ask about the morality of what you see.

✂ **Monitor their YouTube viewing.** Where once there was a watershed, now children can watch anything at any time, thanks to cable, pay-per-view and online on-demand TV. This means they can stumble across unsuitable programming any time of the day or night. The quickest and easiest way to make YouTube kid-friendly is to enable Safety Mode, which will screen out unpleasant content.

✂ **Understand the TV ratings.** Learn what they mean – and stick to them. Point them out to your child to show it's not just you who is looking out for what's safe for them to watch. Consider TV controls that screen out unsuitable material.

- **Make TV a family pastime.** At any given moment, your family may all be on a range of different media, from tablets to computers and telephones. But, although you are all together in your home, you are all alone. Go back to making television a collective, shared experience by holding family movie nights.

- **Be a good role model.** Does your life revolve around who's getting voted off *The X Factor*, *Big Brother*, *The Apprentice* and *Strictly Come Dancing*? If so, you could be passing on the idea that the whole world is there to be judged and criticised. If you are watching these programmes with your children, question how healthy these judgements are and what might be motivating the judges and participants.

FASHION
How clothes don't make the girl

'Our group has to have a definite look. Our hair is long and shiny, sometimes with a fringe swept over to one side. We wear denim shorts with midriff tops and high top trainers. You'd have to be pretty daring to step outside that.'

ELINOR, THIRTEEN

'Whenever I see my thirteen-year-old daughter going out half-dressed in a micro-mini and camisole top, I say: "It looks like you want to have sex." When I tell her, she looks horrified because it's not what she wants. But young girls see so many models and pop stars barely dressed, they just can't see the messages they are sending out by wearing next to nothing. I don't think she really knows why she does it. She just picks up on the idea that it's the right thing to do.'

LUCY, 39

To the pulse of loud pop music, six-year-old Zariah struts down the catwalk in a John Paul Gaultier outfit, best described as a tartan tea cosy with a matching hat and handbag. No matter, because Zariah is, in fashion speak, 'working it'. She sashays to a pink cross on the floor, juts out her hip for the massed ranks of photographers and flounces back to the applause of fashionistas holding up their iPhones to capture the moment. Next up at Global Kids Fashion Week is Benjamin, seven. While other children give gap-toothed grins, Benjamin adopts the exaggerated shoulder sway and far-away look of a male model, just one that's been shrunk in the wash.

On the side-lines, as at any big show, there is a strict hierarchy about who sits where. Naturally the fashion elite, such as sisters Jodie and Jemma Kidd, are in the front row. But this time their most noticeable accessories are not their fabulous shoes or handbags but the impeccably dressed children on their laps.

'So adorable!' trill the fashion pack around me, all eager to know where they can get scaled-up versions of such cute outfits for themselves. After all, what's not to love? The atmosphere is positively bristling with energy as child models, some of whom have taken two days off from school to be here, perform flips and break-dance moves.

Oh so carefully, the organisers have also headed off any accusation that such an event might sexualise young children. There is not even the slightest hint of lip gloss, just a sprinkle of glitter in the girls' hair. Nor are there little ones clacking down the catwalk in mini high heels. Instead, Doc Martens and Mary Janes are the order of the day. Concern about inappropriate clothing in the high street means there are no crop tops either. No, according to the publicity machine, this is all about 'playfulness', 'fun' and 'dressing up'!

But after two days at Global Kids Fashion Week, it took more than a goody bag and a front row seat to convince me that this is just about 'encouraging kids to express their individuality'. There is no doubt the event was a success. Tickets were sold out. Headlines were grabbed around the world. There is already feverish talk of future kids' catwalk shows. But, rather than fall for the glamour because 'it's fashion, *dahling*', we need to step back and take a very long look at the drip-down effect this will have on our children in the long run.

As I remember it, didn't dressing up as a child use to be about pretending to be a medieval knight or a cowboy, not playing at being glamorous, grown-up label slaves? Just because high fashion is cool, it shouldn't conceal the fact that the rise of designer children's brands is nothing more than the commercialisation of childhood. Even before their relentless growth over the last five years, research found that children were starting to recognise logos at the age of eighteen months. By the age of ten, the average child has already memorised 300 to 400 brands. Among eight- to fourteen-year-olds, 92 per cent are specific about which ones they want to buy.

Even before Global Kids Fashion Week, we have increasingly been hearing that children need the right designer labels to make them feel 'special', 'give them confidence', 'make them popular at school' and 'protect them from bullying'. Already the next generation has been experiencing unprecedented levels of anxiety about their bodies, leading to a rise in eating disorders. So, do we really need to be piling on the pressure by allowing our children to believe that they not only need perfect figures, but that they also need exactly the right designer clothes to drape themselves in?

Of course, children's luxury wear is now big business. From a niche market twenty years ago, it is now valued at £6.5 billion in the UK alone, with every major designer, from Chloe to Marc Jacobs, now offering their own children's line. And while the clothes may be small, the price tags are hefty. A new season party dress by one of the designers on display here, Roberto Cavalli, will set you back £350. A pair of baby bootees will cost £90.

Sitting in the front row today is Kayarna, eight. The little girl tells me her style heroine is Rihanna – 'when she has her clothes on', thankfully – so today she is wearing a pair of faux-leather black trousers and a purple gilet from River Island, from the pop star's collection for the company.

Some days, Kayarna tells me she spends up to 25 minutes picking out her outfits, arranging them and accessorising them. Her most prized designer item is a mini Marc Jacobs dress. Designer clothes make her feel 'special', she explains. 'All my friends at school want to learn about them too when I am wearing them. They make me feel like I'm on the catwalk.' Sipping champagne at the after party is a mum, Teodora. She tells me she spends £3,000 a year – more than she spends on herself – kitting out her children, Sienna, eighteen months, and Alex, four – mainly in Ralph Lauren. Although they don't know the value of what they wear, Teodora says it fills her with pride to see them well-dressed – and for others, also in the know, to appreciate the trouble and expense she has been to. Her children are, she admits, 'her trophies'.

Her sister Donna, with whom she co-owns two children's hair salons, blames celebrity culture and mums' one-upmanship for the obsession with designer brands among parents.

'It comes from the mums. We have children in the salon who say they are allergic to carbs because that is what their parents tell them, so of course they are influenced by their parents. Children of three have dresses worth the same as the ones worn by a 30-year-old. It depends on the parents' income. Lots of our clients have an entire wardrobe of designer clothes.'

Today is also a big family day out for Carrie, 25, who has travelled all the way from Bolton to London with her mother, partner and two small daughters for this event. To prove that her baby Lillie really is dressed top to toe in Roberto Cavalli, she lifts up Lillie's frilly dress to show me her bottom, branded with the company symbol on her tights.

Carrie's partner works in security, but money is no object when it comes to dressing their little ones. She regularly spends up to £500 a month on designer children's wear websites, compared to just £50 on her own clothes.

Never mind that she has to make do with jeans and sweatshirts. Carrie is so proud of how her daughters look that she regularly posts their outfits on Facebook. Because of that, she will never dress her baby in hand-me-downs, in case her girls are seen in the same outfit twice.

'When my girls are beautifully dressed, nothing else seems to matter,' says Carrie. 'It's a reflection on me as a parent. It doesn't matter what I wear. People treat you differently when your children are in designer clothes. We go to baby ballet classes, and the ones who know what to look for are a bit nicer and friendlier.'

Though this is imposing adult values on children, there is some good news on the fashion front. Since sexualisation first hit the headlines and governments started to look into its effects, it has been much harder to find T-shirts emblazoned with slogans like 'Future Miss World' or 'I only date millionaires'. The big high street names have woken up to the fact that it's bad PR to use clothing to 'adultify' children.

Abercrombie and Fitch has dropped its 'cute butt' leggings in kids' sizes and Skechers no longer markets shoes to girls as young as eight to help create 'more toned leg and buttock muscles'. Yet some of the vocabulary of children's clothes marketing still remains questionable. Next, for example, still feels the need to call a baggy school cardigan a 'boyfriend cardigan'.

But many people are still making children into designer mini-mes, and we have to be careful of turning them into little billboards to advertise our needs. While it may be fine for companies to sell the idea that wearing designer clothes makes you more special to adults, who should know better, is it fair to sell that dream to children, who are so much more vulnerable and desperate to belong?

Education expert Sue Palmer says she has come across little girls as young as three having tantrums because they didn't get the designer shoes they wanted – which came with mini bags of lip gloss. Even in nursery, Sue says children have already been seduced by the idea that the right brands will make them more popular.

'Fashion, whether it's sexy or not, is an adult concept. Great fun it can be too, as long as one has money to spend or enough self-confidence to enjoy fashion rather than becoming a slave to it.'

'But what's fun for adults and teenagers isn't necessarily good for children. The earlier you are hooked on fashion, the more likely you are to be a fashion victim in the future, desperately searching for an off-the-peg identity rather than developing a fully-rounded personality of your own.'

As the commercialisation of childhood has made parents take leave of their common sense, Sue says our children no longer have clothes in which they can simply be themselves.

'Apart from "best clothes" for special occasions, children need outfits that allow them to play freely: sensible footwear and practical easy-to-clean clothing in which to run, jump, climb and generally mess about.'

WHAT YOU CAN DO

For younger girls

- **Find other ways to make her feel special.** Don't try to show your daughter she is special because of the way she is dressed. Otherwise she will think she is loved for her appearance, and that she is an object to be looked at. Instead, delight in her humour, her capabilities and her character.

- **Don't turn children into mini-mes.** Just because miniature versions of what you wear are available in the children's sections on the high street doesn't make it OK. Little girls have the rest of their lives to wear high heels and camisoles if they choose. Give them the freedom to play unselfconsciously in clothes they don't have to worry about. Tell them how useful their clothes are for climbing trees or letting them run around in wet weather, not how pretty they make them look.

- **Avoid designer labels.** Why would you devalue your child by making her a walking ad for a company's products? Certainly, young children don't know the difference between branded and non-branded clothes unless you make a big deal of it. Get your child to question whether an item of clothing is worth £100 more because it has the letters 'D' and 'G' on it.

- **Agree to compromise.** If your daughter has reached the stage where she will only wear what she wants to wear, don't force her. There are bigger battles to fight. It's probably because she wants to signal her belonging to friendship groups, not because she's showing you a lack of respect. Banning clothes will just make them more alluring to her, so try to find a middle way – why not let her go through a clothing catalogue you both like and give her a budget so you can agree on some outfits? You will feel under less pressure – and there will be fewer rows – than if you go shopping with her.

❈ **Ask schools to think twice about non-uniform days.** Even in primary schools, these can spark a great deal of worry among children anxious to wear the right thing. Ask schools to consider other ways of making money for charity.

How to defy the stereotypes

It's eight o'clock on a freezing Saturday evening in Manchester – but from the skimpy outfits on display, you'd think it was 80° in high summer. Here the teenage girls' hemlines are so high, and their tops so low, that there are no more than a few inches of fabric to shield them from the biting November cold. Only the fake tans manage to hide the goose-bumps as they totter along uncertainly in six-inch 'hooker heels', arm in arm for support.

Of course, there's nothing new or shameful about young women wanting to look attractive on a night out. From the acres of limbs that are exposed, it would be easy to assume that these girls are proud of their bodies. But look deeper and it emerges that attracting leering approaches from men is rather a way to bandage up their insecurities in a world where they can't match up to the oh-so-sexy celebrity stereotypes of womanhood. Scratch the surface and many of these girls are racked with concerns that they are overweight, that their bodies are not good enough and that they are not attractive enough as they are.

With so many young women hating the way they look deep down, provoking lust has simply become the best way they know to make themselves feel better. Only when the night is over will they privately admit it's a relief to return to their daytime wardrobe of comfy tracksuits and UGG boots.

For Sian, an eighteen-year-old carer, her insecurities about showing off her figure are so profound that she admits to drinking spirits with her friend to work up the courage to leave the house for her night out: 'We looked in the mirror before we left the house and we were so upset, we necked half a bottle of vodka each.'

Her friend Beth, a student, is wearing suspender-style tights, made popular by celebrities like Rihanna. She didn't buy them to look cutting edge, but to cover up her legs, which she describes as 'vile'. 'I feel there's lots of pressure to look good. Boys always want that perfect person and other women all look amazing.'

When Amber, eighteen, goes out, she wears her full armoury of push-up bra and false eyelashes. But she has the self-knowledge to realise that ultimately it's not a very convincing mask:

'The only problem is that this isn't what we really look like. In the morning, you'd be there without your hair extensions, make-up and false eyelashes, or your body control pants, and you'd look completely different. Nobody knows what you really look like when you're dressed up like this.'

The ubiquitous sky-high heels are also about trying to create an illusion of perfection. Trisha, 22, admits she wears six-inch heels to go out because 'without them, my legs look fatter – they make you taller and make you tense your bum more so you look better ...The more glam your outfit is, the less people look at your figure.'

When it comes to X-rated dressing, there are also many formulas in place, although the underlying principle is simply: 'If you've got it, flaunt it.' As Eleanor, seventeen, explains: 'If you have legs out, then no tits. If you have tits out, no legs.' Another general rule girls this age live by is, 'the higher the heel, the more confi-dent you are'. Body parts are also traded. Women describe using their legs and cleavage to distract from less-than-flat stomachs.

But the price is not just to these young women's self-esteem, but also to their bodies. They are willing to go through agony to spend the evening walking around in high heels, and girls report coming home with feet bloodied from blisters. But still the pain is worth it to look taller and thinner.

Kelly, 22, says: 'My highest heels are six or seven inches – I can walk around all night in most of them. Of course it hurts, but I think it's worth it. If you want to look good, beauty is pain.'

Even if she is freezing as she walks between pubs and clubs, she says she just drinks more. 'The drink warms you up by the end of the night.'

Wanting to be desired and complimented is understandable. But we need to ask why these girls need the compliments they hope these outfits will attract – and why men scorn them for trying so hard. To the male bystanders they dress for, it's simply convenient to have a meat market of flesh on show. Other men we spoke to described the women as 'eye candy for free' and a chance to 'window shop'.

The reason 29-year-old Toby, a project manager, says he likes women dressing in barely-there clothes is 'because you get to think whether you want to sleep with them later. It's a certain sort of woman who dresses that way – easy chicks. They're definitely not a long-term prospect because they are easy. They're dressing for men and to get attention. I'd rather be accepted by my male peers than women.'

For Lewis, 23, 'being around all these women is like being at a funfair with flaring lights in your face – but they're not the sort I go for as it's too revealing for me. They dress like that because they want to go back home with a man. My ideal woman would be someone you can take to see your mum – someone I could feel comfortable with and trust not to be wearing a mini-skirt which flashes her underwear at my parents. I think it's sexier to put a nice long dress on.'

When I look back at pictures of myself at university, if there was a mini-skirt in sight, it was muted with woolly tights or baggy jumpers. We wore huge men's overcoats and scarves. Yet my daughter's friends, although several years younger, will sometimes turn up in midriff-exposing tops with tummies fully on display, buttock-skimming shorts and playsuits that look like lingerie, which makes we wonder if we've just stopped noticing how much has changed.

In younger girls, this is mostly artless: worn to fit in with cliques. Yet I don't think it's prudish to point out that I would have felt a lot more comfortable in my standard student outfit than my daughter's friends seem to in theirs, when they have to keep pulling their tops down over their tummies, and working hard to keep their boobs in their bras when they lean over. But then, by the time your daughter is a teen, she is likely to have been so desensitised to seeing pop stars walking around in little more than their underwear, she may honestly think she's fully dressed in next to nothing. Even so, their self-consciousness is plain to see.

Our daughters are now so worried about what they wear that a recent survey found that a half of girls have been put off sport purely because the kit was too ugly. So let's remind our daughters that clothes are not just meant to highlight the most attractive parts of our bodies to men. They can also change the way we behave, how we perceive our bodies, and hinder us rather than help us to live the life we want.

WHAT YOU CAN DO

❋ **Talk about the message of clothes.** Talk about how clothes can prevent her using her body fully and can turn it into something to be looked at rather than to be used. Demonstrate how stilt-like heels stop girls running and make them helpless. Get her to question whether boys would put themselves through agony like this to make their bodies look 'better'.

❋ **Tell her where fashion comes from.** Fashion has become an increasingly throwaway pastime, with girls often only wearing cheap items once or twice before claiming they have nothing to wear. Before it gets to that stage, teach your daughter awareness of how cheap clothes are made, and the human cost of sweatshops.

❋ **Ask her to think how other people will view her.** If your daughter wants to go out in something that you feel looks provocative, don't scream and shout. If you prohibit her, she'll only sneak the outfit out of the house and put it on at her friend's house. Instead, ask her how she thinks she will be perceived. Tell her you understand she wants to look more mature, but explain that while she thinks she looks cool, some people, whose attentions she may not welcome, may think she wants sex. It may not change her mind, but at least you've made her aware of the impression she might be creating.

❋ **Tone it down.** If, as is the fashion nowadays, girls insist on wearing micro shorts and crop tops, suggest she customises them with leggings or camisoles underneath. If she is wearing her clothes to look part of her group, rather than appear sexy, she may not mind if she still keeps her overall look. Keep explaining that it's not that you don't like her style, but you want to make sure she feels comfortable.

FINDING GOOD ROLE MODELS

'As a teacher, I have come across girls in my class who look at Colleen Rooney and have said, "Oh, I'd just love her lifestyle" – and they really mean it. When I've had to talk to other girls about their work, I've also heard, "Don't worry, Miss. I can marry a footballer" – and they're only half joking. Seeing people become famous through no talent has definitely contributed to a something-for-nothing culture in schools. Some kids think they don't have to work as hard because somehow they'll find a way to get it all to land in their laps.'

LOUISE, 29

'When I started writing an agony aunt column fifteen years ago, I would get letters from girls asking how to be doctors and scientists. Now I'm getting letters from girls who say they want to be famous, but don't know how because there's nothing they're good at.'

AGONY AUNT HILARY FREEMAN

Considering the advances that women have made over the last two generations, it's telling that 42 per cent of girls name celebrities as their greatest influences. Kim Kardashian, Colleen Rooney and Kate Middleton are some of the role models that many girls look up to. While boys admire sports stars, these women are chiefly worshipped for being size ten or less, being beautiful or for who they are married to. It has got to the point where women can base entire careers on one part of their body. For Kim Kardashian, it was her bottom. For Katie Price, it was her breasts.

In a climate where new celebrities are elevated from obscurity by reality TV shows, girls often believe that wealth and fame can be achieved overnight by meeting the right man or landing a part on the right programme. With the rare exception of young women like Malala Yousafzai, who was shot in the head at the age of thirteen for campaigning for girls' education in Pakistan and continues to campaign for it, there are precious few other girls or women who are feted in the media solely for their intelligence or integrity.

The messages that girls take away from these examples are many and varied. While most girls admire the fact these well-known women look in control, they also conclude that who you marry will enhance your wealth and status, and that a good body means you are more successful. Seven in ten teachers now believe that celebrity culture is perverting children's aspirations and encouraging a generation to believe you can be successful without hard work.

As mothers, our daughter's first female role model should be us. If we get it right, we can model perseverance, wisdom, empathy and self-acceptance, no matter what we achieve in life. But beyond that, we are not fulfilling our roles as parents if we do not encourage our girls to raise their eyes higher to prominent women who are known for their determination, hard work and strength.

WHAT YOU CAN DO

❈ **Ask them what they admire about their role model.** If they attach themselves to a particular celebrity, make sure they don't just worship them blindly. Encourage a balanced view by asking them what characteristics are really important and helping them to see a bigger picture.

❈ **Don't hero worship.** As a parent, putting celebrities on pedestals and avidly following their fortunes belittles you and gives famous people more importance than they deserve. No one is superhuman. Don't make your child feel any less special than the people she sees on TV and in magazines.

❈ **Make your own role models close to home.** Help girls look beyond the cult of youth and celebrity and praise the people that you know personally for their kindness and generosity.

MATERIAL GIRLS

How to fight back against
the pressure to buy

Twelve-year-old Louise only got her last phone – her third in two years – six months ago, but already she is complaining that her latest model is running out of storage and she needs an upgrade. The iPad she got for her eleventh birthday also doesn't have the latest camera, so she has already started her stealth campaign for the latest version in time for Christmas.

In a few weeks' time it's the start of school. But Louise won't just need a new uniform. The really important items – the ones that other girls will notice when she turns up – will be her new Ice watch, as only the most popular girls have them. Then she needs a trendy pencil case to put in the front pocket of the right school bag.

Louise's mum, Jo, recently bought her daughter some new trainers. But then one of her friends said they 'looked a bit weird from the back', so now Louise is counting down the days until Saturday when she can go with her mum to the shops again to the get the 'right ones'. Jo – who works to keep up their family lifestyle – can't really afford yet another pair. Given that her daughter now takes an adult size, it's a substantial investment.

But she'll get them for her anyway. Jo knows all too well that the right brand names are important to help her daughter fit in. There's also the fact that Jo thinks their best bonding time (code for when Louise behaves because she's getting what she wants) is when they spend a girlie afternoon at the shopping centre, just the two of them.

Children are influenced by marketing from as young as eighteen months, when they start recognising logos. By the age of two, they can even match them with the right products. Buying this must-have stuff has become necessary for us to feel we are good parents. Our children have become our family's brand ambassadors.

Beyond this, it's much more serious than children just being spoilt. Part of the reason childhood is being eroded is that young girls are being seen as a lucrative new market now the rising number of working parents has the money to pay for these goods. The result is that everywhere they go, children are inundated with consumer messages. Marketing messages pop up on mobile phones. Ads appear as banners at the top, sides and bottoms of websites, or jump out of them on screen, uninvited, as pop-ups.

The issue with aiming products at young people is that they don't have the discrimination to pick and choose. Up to the age of seven, children accept everything advertising and marketers tell them without question. Even when they are old enough to know they are being flogged something, they still fall for the notion that they need products to make them look cooler.

Of course, it still takes a big person to pay for them. As parents, we too get caught up with the fear that if we don't get our child an Xbox, Wii, iPod or iPad, they will lose out. Because so many activities are based around computers and consoles, parents start to believe that their children *have* to have these things in order to play together. In one US study, 58 per cent of nine- to fourteen-year-olds said they felt the pressure to buy stuff to belong – and they are certainly not going to tell their parents otherwise.

Here in the UK, it's the families least able to afford it who are affected most. Peer pressure has become so acute that one study found that children from poorer homes in this country said they had no interest in talking to other youngsters who weren't wearing the most fashionable trainers.

So we keep buying to show we care – and to be good parents. A recent survey found that the average teenage bedroom has become a treasure trove, containing £5,257 worth of gadgets, games and gear. The huge sum includes about £1,700 of the latest electrical equipment, £1,000 of clothes and £250 of trainers. On the poorest council estates, parents end up putting themselves in debt because they don't know how to fight pester power for the latest phones and game consoles.

After all, how can we say no? Our adult lives are also filled with gadgets, from flat screen TVs to iPads, that prove how up-to-date we are. Consumer culture has become part of our family identity.

Of course, to begin with the consumer world is fun for kids. But the more hooked they get, the more it leads to unrealistic expectations and disappointment. The more ads children see, the more they know what's out there and the more they think they need. And even when they get what they think they want, children don't stay happy. The more brands children know about, the more dissatisfied they are with their lives and the more they are set up for a life of what *Toxic Childhood* author Sue Palmer refers to as 'consumer driven unhappiness'.

For girls, the problem can be even more acute because they usually need a wider range of the 'right clothes' to fit in with their friendship group. Advertising creates the powerful expectation that there is fashion, products and make-up out there which can 'fix' what's wrong with them, or make them more desirable to their peers. But girls who hate their hair, for example, and want Cheryl Cole's dazzling mane of chestnut curls will find that despite the glossy ad pictures, the L'Oréal shampoo they use won't do the same for them. That's because if you read the fine print, you'll see that Cheryl is wearing expensive hair extensions.

So, don't let advertising create a void in your daughter that can never be filled. Teach her how to reject the marketers' messages and that, above all, she is more than the sum of what she owns.

WHAT YOU CAN DO

For younger kids

- **Talk to your daughter about advertising.** Advertisers know that in order to sell a product, they have to make a consumer feel she is not good enough without it – and persuade her that their product will fix her problem. Remind her that big businesses have profits, not their customers' well-being, at heart, whatever PR spin they put on it.

- **Give time, not things.** More than ever, it's not material goods our girls need from us, but one-on-one, uninterrupted, technology-free time. The more gifts we shower them with to compensate for our absence, the more children come to associate happiness with wanting things, buying things and having things bought for them. Instead, show love by going on walks together. Have no-buy days when you make a point of having fun without spending a single penny.

- **Be a good role model.** Girls learn consumer habits from their parents. So, moderate your own need to buy and don't pin your hopes of happiness on your next purchase. Go shopping because you need things, not to cheer yourself up.

※ **Use ads as a first step towards media awareness.** When teaching children not to accept everything they see without question, start with ads. They're a quick way to teach media literacy because they're brief and it's easy for kids to understand how biased they are. From there, it will be easier to move on to TV, movies and websites.

※ **Don't buy into brands.** Teach girls early that brands are more about perception than reality. Try this experiment. Buy a box of brand name cornflakes and the supermarket own brand version, and ask your daughter to spot the differences in the ingredients. She will find that they are essentially the same product – except the one with the well-known name is substantially more expensive.

※ **Add up the ads.** Go through a magazine and play a game of adding up everything advertised to show them how much a real consumer would have to fork out if they bought everything they were told to.

※ **Don't make shopping your main family activity.** For many mothers and daughters, shopping can easily become their main bonding activity. Instead, find other activities – like visiting a museum or art gallery – to keep you close.

※ **Don't start kids on collectables.** Don't encourage an addiction to merchandise and commercial toy sets that create endless demands for more accessories. The only winners here will be the manufacturers who deliberately set out to create pester power.

✷ **Talk about fads and crazes.** Letting fads take hold can be an expensive business – and within a few months, once the moment has passed, you can be left with loads of items your child now won't look at twice. Talk about the crazes that came and went in your childhood – like Rubik's cubes or Pokémon – to show how fleeting trends are.

✷ **Play 'I spy' with packaging.** On a visit to a supermarket, my girls and I counted 50 different cartoon characters on food packages, from Homer Simpson to Dora the Explorer. On your next visit, make it a game for your daughter to spot the characters, to help make her more media-savvy about the way food manufacturers try to make her buy.

✷ **Watch ad-free TV.** Don't leave your child in front of a TV churning out a constant stream of ads. With younger children, one of the best ways to screen them out is to stick to non-commercial television, like CBeebies, for as long as possible – or stick to a library of DVDs fast-forwarded through the commercials.

✷ **Make a complaint.** The Advertising Standards Authority is there for good reason – and all you need to do is fill in a four-step email form if you come across something you think takes advantage of children. It can take just one complaint for the ASA to launch an investigation, which is often all it takes for an inappropriate ad to be withdrawn.

✷ **Use your parent power.** Remember that most major companies don't want to be officially censored for being irresponsible towards children. They might be tempted to risk a bit of controversy to get attention, but if it looks like they are being irresponsible with the welfare of children, it doesn't look good.

WHAT YOU CAN DO

For older girls

✳ **Point out the small print.** As girls get older and worry more about their looks, they are more tempted by the allure of beauty ads. Tell your daughter to check the small print to make it clear how fake some of these images are. If she shows an interest in diet aids, tell her to make a game of looking for get-outs like: 'Only use as part of a calorie-controlled diet.'

✳ **Keep talking.** Talk to your daughter about where the products we buy come from, how they got here and issues like ethical trading and fair trade. Explain that there is a human and environmental cost to endless consumerism.

HOW TO 'UNSPOIL' CHILDREN

It's not just make-up and clothes that make little girls seem older than they are. An obsession with shopping, designer brands and the latest 'in' thing – whether it's clothes, gadgets or make-up – can also replace innocence with a grasping precociousness in our daughters.

The problem with giving our children everything is that it's never, ever enough. The more you give them, the more they want – and the less they will appreciate it. As loving parents, so often we grant them their heart's desire, thinking that will finally make them happy, only to find they quickly move on to wanting something else. With the proliferation of new products coming on the market all the time, there will always be something else they want, unless you put the brakes on children's insatiable desire to consume.

Consumerism makes girls prioritise superficial things in a life and steals away what's really important. One unpleasant side effect is that parents who thought they were doing the right thing by providing materially for their children find they have ended up with spoilt brats. But even if you realise it's gone too far, it's not too late.

WHAT YOU CAN DO

❋ **Ask yourself why you are spoiling them.** As much as we hate to admit it, part of the reason our children crave so much is because we give them too much – without setting any limits. While it's true that marketers are out to attract them, it's you who's actually paying up. So first, work out why you feel the need to overindulge your kids. Is it because you work long hours and feel guilty? Are you afraid your child won't love you if you say no? Or are you so busy trying to make your child's life perfect, you forgot to set restrictions? Or maybe you want them to have more than you did as kid? It's only once you've worked out your own reasons that you're ready to change your child's behaviour.

❋ **Check your kids aren't your status symbols.** Check that you're not allowing your daughters to have the latest things as an outward display to your peers that you are a loving – but also affluent – parent. If so, restrain your spending, so that the message that material things are important doesn't rub off on your girls.

❋ **Make them earn it.** If you give treats to children all the time, they won't thank you. Instead they'll just take it for granted and want something new the next day. Girls should earn privileges, because they'll automatically respect things more when they have to work for them and will also appreciate them more when they get them.

❊ **Explain how it's going to change.** Half-hearted attempts to unspoil children won't work. You have to work at it, and make sure your partner is on the same wavelength as you, as kids are experts at playing parents off against each other. If you feel it's gone too far, it's not too late to draw a line in the sand. Choose a quiet, neutral time – in other words when your child is not asking for anything – to explain to your daughter that money does not come easily and fun things need to be earned. Listen carefully to your child's questions and try to answer them. You might have to strap yourself in for a few tantrums, but stick to your rules.

❊ **Don't fall for: 'It's unfair!' Don't let your child bribe you with claims that it's not fair when you don't buy her what she wants.** Parenting educator Noël Janis-Norton of Calmer, Easier, Happier Parenting says: 'Children don't really understand the concept of fairness. What they really mean is "I don't like what you're saying" or "I thought I'd be getting something you're not going to give me." Many of our children are among the most privileged in the Western world, so that's not fair either.'

❊ **Remember gadgets won't make kids cleverer.** Many parents shower their kids with the latest educational toys, gadgets and puzzles because they think it will aid their intellectual development. But it won't be the educational apps on your iPad or the computer learning games that will make your daughter excel. It will be the amount of time you spend with her, explaining how the world works.

※ **Resist pester power.** Many mums and dads buy kids new things because they think they'll get left out at school if they don't have the latest fad. If you really think they might suffer, check it's something you want them to have. Offer them a taster first to see if that satisfies their curiosity. If they're still desperate, tell them they can still earn it with extra jobs around the house or by saving up their allowance.

※ **Drip-feed presents.** Many mums know the embarrassment of watching kids opening present after present at birthdays and Christmases, and barely looking up to say thank you before moving on to the next gift. So, at a quiet time, explain there will be a new rule that gifts will be spaced out throughout the year. Set limits by asking friends and relatives to give just one gift on special occasions, and to donate anything else they really want to give to your child's savings account.

※ **Encourage charity and voluntary work.** Teach kids that it's not just receiving that makes them feel good. Giving does too. Steer their priorities away from consumer culture by taking your child along to help with voluntary work at a charity to teach them that others are not as lucky as they are.

TOYS
Want to play sexy ladies?

'My friend played with Barbies, but then she cut all
their hair off and threw them in the bin. I don't like
them either. It looks funny that she's got a little girl's
face on the body of a stick lady with pointy boobs.'

TASHA, SIX

'My daughter loves Bratz dolls. She likes their style,
and they have really funky clothes. She role plays them
competing in *The X Factor* and going in for competitions.'

MICHELLE, 34

At the five-star Forte Village Resort in Sardinia, girls as young as two can enjoy Barbie VIP packages, which include learning how to walk on the runway, having spa treatments and being made up with 'glamorous make-up and hairstyling'. In another package, girls aged four to eleven can enjoy the Barbie Premium Experience with the world's biggest cruise company, Royal Caribbean, offering a 'Barbie dream cruise complete with fun, fashion and runway moments'.

A visit to the dolls aisle at Toys "R" Us is a bracing lesson in what our little girls are supposed to be interested in these days. Dolls are essential to child development because they help children see their own place in the world. But if these playthings are anything to go by, our children can look forward to a life in barely-there clothing and high heels, with a mobile phone glued to one hand and a powder compact glued to the other. Step back, if you can adjust your eyes to the blinding sugary pink around you, and think about the messages these toys are sending to girls.

Apart from a few dolls wearing skinny jeans, the rest are in skirts, and there is not one dressed in a skirt that reaches below the top of her skinny plastic thighs. All their outfits look more suited to a strip club than a children's playroom. Compared to her successors – Bratz, Moxie Girls and Monster High range – Barbie now looks like a natural beauty, even with her sexually mature body and adult face.

To make these new dolls even more 'realistic', marketers have also created vacuous lives for them that can be lived out in cyber-space. Bratz dolls, Chloe, Sasha, Jade and Yasmin, all have blogs in which it is their avowed intention to become famous and go shopping.

When I wrote the first edition of this book, dolls were one of the things that fiercely divided mothers. On the one hand, there was unanimous agreement that it was not a good idea to dress four-year-olds in hot pants, high heels and boob tubes. Yet at the same time, mothers defended to the hilt their right to give their girls dolls dressed exactly the same way. As one mum told me: 'I played with Barbies, and I'm not a Page Three girl.'

But just because your child can't become a living doll, doesn't mean she doesn't get the idea she should look like one. Mattel claims that one in three little girls owns a Barbie, and Barbie is the stereotype that comes up again and again when young girls are asked to say who they would like to look like. When one study showed 200 girls aged five to eight pictures of Barbie, versus a doll who represented a more realistic body shape, the results were stark. After seeing Barbie, girls were more dissatisfied with their own shape and aspired to more extreme thinness. For those aged six to seven, the negative effects were even stronger.

In fact, Barbie has become so much of a symbol of the stereotypical way women should look, she even her has own disorder – 'Barbie syndrome' – which describes women with a pathological need to get her unrealistic body shape. These young women are putting their bodies through punishing regimes of exercise and plastic surgery to make sure they look like caricatures of womanhood – which they hold up as the paragon of man-pleasing beauty.

It's not just looks, but aspirations that are affected. One study found that girls who play with Barbie dolls have a narrower outlook on career possibilities for women. In one study, 37 young girls between the ages of four and seven were randomly assigned to play with either a fashion Barbie, a career-driven doctor Barbie or a 'more neutral' Mrs Potato Head for ten minutes. The girls were then shown photographs of ten jobs and asked how many they themselves or boys could do in the future. The girls who played with a Barbie doll – irrespective of whether it was a 'fashion' or 'career' Barbie – saw themselves as able to do fewer occupations than boys could, while the ones who played with Mrs Potato Head said they could try just as many.

Dr Helen Nightingale of the British Psychological Association says it's the gap between the age represented by the dolls and the age of the children who play with them that is part of the problem with these types of doll.

'When Barbies were designed half a century ago, they were probably meant for thirteen- and fourteen-year-olds, not the three- and four-year-olds who get given them now. But it's not just about the dolls we buy our children. It's the values we impart to them when we give them to girls. After all, dolls are passive objects. So, for example, if a parent gives the impression that

Barbie is sexy or this is how they think their daughters should aspire to look, that's the real message the child learns.'

As Natasha Walter says in her book Living Dolls: 'The strange melding of the doll and the real girls can continue way beyond childhood. When the singers in Girls Aloud launched Barbie doll versions of themselves, you could look – to paraphrase George Orwell – from doll to girl and girl to doll, and it was almost impossible to see which was which.'

WHAT YOU CAN DO

* **Give girls dolls that are representative or beyond comparison.** Whatever kids are surrounded by they consider normal, and that includes dolls with prominent breasts and tiny waists. Either give your daughter dolls with childlike features or ones that can't be compared to the human form – like rag dolls. Then let her make up her own mind about who these dolls are and how to play with them.

* **Talk about what dolls do.** If your little girl just loves Barbies, Moxie Girlz or Bratz, discuss what she likes about them. Ask her if she has ever met a woman who looks like one in real life. Tell her all the things that Barbie wouldn't be able to do if she were a real woman because her feet are arched permanently for high heels. Suggest games where Barbie becomes a scientist or a politician.

* **Buy basic toys.** Don't buy toys from movie franchises where the scripts are already written. Allow your daughter to use her imagination to create her own play worlds. Stick with the basics by buying kids simple playthings so they have to use their creativity.

QUIZZES AND GAMES

One of the simplest and most enjoyable ways to help your daughter enjoy her childhood is to play games with her. Rather than allowing her to play solitary games on her computer, or allowing her life to be taken over by an obsession with fashion or make-up, give her the companionship and interaction she needs in the form of board games and quizzes. Here are some games that I have found particularly good for younger girls:

Star cards. This is a box of 52 cards, with descriptions like 'loving', 'patient' and 'honest', which help children get to know themselves and recognise their inner qualities. For information, go to www.relaxkids.com.

The awkward question game. Get communication going by asking each other tricky questions – and answering honestly so you get to know each other better.

Mind-mapping. This is a great idea adapted from a concept by Tony Buzan. Get kids to draw themselves or write their name in the middle of the page and branch off into all the things that are important about them. You may find at first they define themselves by the toys and gadgets they own. Instead, show them how to think of themselves in terms of the qualities they possess, like humour and loyalty.

Talk about each other's childhoods. Few things make a daughter's ears prick up more than when you share stories about your experiences as a child. Tell her about your early life and how it compares with or differs from her own.

Argue with your daughter. Choose a topic to debate. Debating helps girls see an argument from both sides, form their views and see that a difference of opinion doesn't have to lead to a row. It also helps them develop a voice with which to speak up.

Play 'Would you rather?' Make up a string of funny dilemmas like, 'Would you rather be the Queen of England or the Prime Minister?' to help her stretch her imagination and think about her priorities.

Let your children play outdoors. Just five minutes of 'green exercise' can make your child feel better about themselves, according to a study from the University of Essex. By letting children get to grips with nature, they see themselves in the context of the wider world. Climbing trees also teaches children how to take responsibility and measure risk.

Build a family tree. Teach your child about her roots to help build her sense of her place in the bigger picture. Make it real for her by adding photographs of ancestors on the branches.

Make a time capsule. Show girls how they can put together some of the things that are important to them here and now. Collect objects like photos, newspaper cuttings and notes about their likes and dislikes. Then seal it in a safe place and open it in five years' time.

Use The Art of Conversation cards. This is a set of 100 conversation builders for kids that can help you find out their opinions on subjects you may never have asked them about. For information, go to www.taoc.com.au.

Make a 'me collage'. Help girls think about who they are and what they like by cutting out pictures of the things they value and creating a collage that sums up who they are and what interests them.

Put together a treasure box. One of the most meaningful gifts a child can have is a keepsake box. Let her fill it with christening or naming day gifts, heirlooms, special mementos or cards. A child will go back to it again and again. It will help her to remember how treasured and loved she is.

HARASSMENT, MISOGYNY AND ABUSE

Keeping girls physically safe

One of the most direct and worrying consequences of how the modern world sees women is the rising number of girls being harassed – and at an earlier age. According to Holly Kearl, author of *Stop Street Harassment*, by the age of twelve, 22 per cent of girls have already had to deal with being sexually bullied on the street.

Much of this harassment is done by insecure males who have seen so many thousands of porn videos, they make the mistake of thinking all women are ready and willing to be used for sex. Seeing so much of this material, viewed on a scale that has never been experienced before in human history, has encouraged a sense of entitlement that has not yet been sufficiently publicly challenged for them to realise that this is wrong. While such messages have always been around in some form, in previous eras it was also assumed that stricter moral codes about sex before marriage meant a woman probably wouldn't agree to sex even if she were asked – in other words, a man was simply trying his luck. But the delusion of porn is that there are no holds barred anymore. In this mindset, every woman must want sex, because there are no reasons not to. As a result, when girls and women assert themselves in real life as individuals, they face increasing vitriol.

As Durham University Criminology professor Nicole Westmarland points out: 'If you didn't have the culture of expectation in the first place, you wouldn't have the culture of rejection. It's all bound to the idea that women are sexual objects for men to do with what they want. Most men aren't thinking like that but some certainly are.'

While most adult women have been subjected to street harassment, they at least have the perspective and resilience to attempt to brush it off. But now there is also the issue of how young the girls are that men make these sexually bullying remarks to.

Men have always been attracted to younger looking girls because of the fantasy that they are corruptible and they have so little experience of the world. In other words, they don't know any better, or might be flattered by the attention. These men also get off more on the fact that younger girls are panicked about what to do. Add to that the toxic proliferation of barely legal porn videos featuring girls of questionable age in school uniform, and you soon see why some males think schoolgirls are fair game.

Yet, as I found out when my own daughter rang me in floods of tears from the train station when she was sexually approached by a man at a bus stop, our girls are not being given the resources to deal with this emerging problem. I certainly had not addressed it with her when she started commuting to school because I didn't want to frighten her. But the incident made me realise that it's essential we parents find an age-appropriate way to tell girls how to handle such behaviour, because they lack the life experience to know what to do for themselves.

WHAT YOU CAN DO

- **Tell them it's unacceptable.** Explain to your girl that she should never have to face harassment in the first place – whether on the street, at school or at a party. Tell her some men have not been taught to respect women in the way that they should and that they have grown up with the wrong expectations because of what they have seen on the internet.

- **Point out the difference between a compliment and a catcall.** In a culture where girls are brought up to seek affirmation of their looks, it is confusing when a man says something flattering to them on the street. Help her understand the difference between a compliment – something said with consideration and respect from someone they know – and a catcall, which is a power play by a strange male to get a female to react. For her own safety, teach her to ignore them.

- **Explain why some males do it.** There are many reasons why a girl may be harassed on the street. Some men are showing off in front of other males, some may be trying to prove they are straight or some may simply be bored and view a passing female as entertainment. Whatever the reason, tell your daughter it's a form of bullying meant to intimidate and make the bully feel more powerful. Explain to your daughter that her body is not public property on show for judgements and comment.

- **Help her work out what to do.** Faced with this intimidation – being approached, followed or curb-crawled – young girls will understandably panic because they have not yet developed the resources or experience to know what to do to counter it.

So give her a drill she can put into place without thinking about it, such as not engaging with them by answering back or making eye contact, and walking towards a busy place or into a shop.

✄ **Tell her who to turn to for help – and how to do it.** If she wants the independence to walk home from school, she has to be able to stop to ask for assistance. Role play a form of asking for help if she gets into a sticky situation. If she is followed, ask her to approach a woman who may be more likely to understand her situation. Or tell her to go into a shop and ask for help at the counter.

✄ **Find a self-defence class.** This is not purely so she can fight back, although it's an important skill, but also to give her the bearing and confidence that will deter men from believing it's easy to make her a victim.

✄ **Tell her to act on her instincts.** Children think they should always be polite to adults – but tell her if something looks or feels wrong, then it probably is, and she does not have to wait around to find out.

✄ **Teach girls the victim is never to blame.** Humiliation and name-calling, and beyond that, rape, are NOT committed because a man is unable to control his lust or attraction. These are crimes about power and violence. Men are perfectly able to control their behaviour if they choose.

✄ **Tell her she is entitled to make a fuss.** Harassment and unwelcome sexual touching is not a compliment. If she rejects it vociferously, she has not 'lost her sense of humour'. She is not being 'oversensitive', and she does not need to 'chill out'.

All these are lines trotted out to silence women about harassment. Don't let these kinds of remark confuse or minimise her reaction. Tell her to reject them outright.

Keeping girls safe from abusers

The targeting of young girls by gangs of youths for sex – and the sort of predation seen in the recent cases of Jimmy Savile and Rolf Harris – is one of the most pressing concerns for parents of girls. The situation is not helped by the huge number of videos on the net showing gang sex, which send out still unhealthier messages that group intercourse with girls is a legitimate hobby for men. All of this is horrifying for parents who, thanks to girls' excellent secret-keeping skills, often have no idea of what their daughters might be caught up in.

The easiest targets for abuse will always be girls with low self-esteem, looking for someone to flatter and 'protect' them – and who find out too late the flip side of the deal.

But even if you feel your daughter does not fall into this category – and even if she is never threatened with violence or rape – you will still be providing her with a lifetime of insight if you show her how to tell the difference between a healthy and an unhealthy relationship. Don't leave it too late. Even though it can be difficult for parents, girls are getting into romantic relationships sooner than ever.

Controlling behaviour can start at any age, so start having the conversation as soon as you notice she's taking an interest in the opposite sex that might lead to a relationship. Even relatively young teenage boys, egged on by brutal pornography, can try to assume dominant positions. Just as you can teach your daughter the difference between a good friend and a bad friend in the playground from the checklist earlier in this book, discuss the difference between a good and a bad 'romantic' relationship.

Even if she never comes across anyone like this, forewarned is forearmed. Above all, spell it out that you are her safety net, and whatever relationships she gets involved in or however embarrassing the outcome, she should never feel too ashamed or frightened to come to you.

Former probation officer Pat Craven tours the country talking to young girls in schools. In her work, she points out the warning signs that will enable girls to spot 'dominators' – not only in grooming gangs, but in everyday relationships. It's far from just being about whether a girl gets raped or physically abused. If a boyfriend makes her feel uneasy, makes her keep secrets or sulks to get his own way, then tell your daughter she should walk away, rather than be dragged in deeper. It's fundamental that we as parents don't also feed our girls myths that can be turned against them, says Pat, like princess stories that teach girls that their place is to be protected and showered with material things. The flip side to these stories is that girls become controlled and are made to feel they 'owe' something. Pat says: 'Young girls are falling into a pattern because they are still getting the message that it's a woman's place to be dominated by a man. For example, don't let them think it's romantic for their boyfriend to be texting 40 times a day.'

As girls get older and start to learn more about adult relationships, it's key for your daughter to be trained to decipher good relationships and bad ones.

Pat says: 'Print out the list of differences between "Mr Wrong" and "Mr Right", stick it on the fridge and ask them to work it out. But unless we show young girls the warning signs, we could be letting them sleepwalk into bad relationships with a lifetime of consequences.'

MISOGYNY

This is a tough one to tackle, but we are living in a society where hatred of women is on the rise. The proliferation of misogynistic websites is just the tip of the iceberg.

Psychologist John Woods of the Portman Clinic in North London told me he has witnessed first-hand how pornography has led to the expansion of woman-hating feelings and believes porn is shaping boys' views of what women should look like, and how they should behave sexually.

'I hear young boys routinely refer to girls as "bitches" who need to be dominated. They bemoan the fact that they can't go out with "real" girls because they want things. In other words, females who exist outside of cyberspace have needs of their own that boys resent having to consider.'

No parent wants to live in a society where girls who have done nothing 'wrong' except for being born female, are treated with hostility. But unless we tell our older girls how to spot misogyny, they are less equipped to fight it and are more likely to be taken by surprise by it.

Of course, misogyny has been with us since the story of Adam and Eve. But in the last few years, there has been an explosion of a particularly violent and virulent form, as evidenced by Elliot Rodger, 22, who in 2014 went on a rampage in California to kill all women, because he felt rejected by just one. Misogyny of this kind has exploded again because some men, who have got used to a sense of entitlement to every woman's body from porn, get very angry when they are rejected by real women – and then club together on websites to make themselves feel that their views are normal. When women are turned into objects on such a mass scale, one woman becomes every woman.

Explain to your daughter that for no good reason, some people learn to hate certain things – either through ignorance, conditioning or as a defence mechanism. Sometimes these people stick together to make them feel justified. Underline that this never makes what they say true. Tell her about the human brain's tendency to stereotype, and compare misogyny to racism. Help her to listen out for these stereotypes. One of the first and most obvious clues that a man is a misogynist is that he will talk in generalised terms about 'all' women or 'all' girls. Tell her that a misogynist will often make references to a woman's looks before anything else – and sort women into categories like bimbos, dumb blondes, gold-diggers or ball-breakers. Teach her to avoid anyone who talks down to her on the basis of her gender. On her own, she won't be able to help him, but she can protect herself.

FEMINISM

Teaching your daughter the F-word

'Parents are always nagging about girls wearing skimpy
clothing. But maybe they should be raising their boys not
to think that girls are objects who are always up for it.'

ARIADNE, FIFTEEN

'It's like saying: "I don't really believe in cars, but
I drive one every day and I love that it gets me
places and makes life so much easier and faster
and I don't know what I would do without it."'

**AMY POEHLER, ON FEMALE STARS
WHO DENY BEING FEMINIST**

As a five-year-old, I can still remember when watching the
Miss World pageant was one of the TV highlights of the year.
Because no one told me any different, when I saw the pretty
ladies up on stage modelling swimsuits and crowned with tiaras,
I thought that must be the pinnacle of achievement for a woman.
I clearly remember telling my father: 'I want to be Miss World
when I grow up.'

But as I did grow, I also became aware of the demonstrations
that surrounded the event. Seeing others protesting opened my
eyes to the fact that women should not be judged and given
marks out of ten, like prize heifers. As a result, I changed my
mind about what I wanted to be – and hoped for more for

myself. Thanks to protests like these, women did start to get equal rights in the workplace – and it looked as if the battle was being won.

When they first appeared in the eighties, symbols such as the conical bras worn by Madonna started to make sex seem empowering to women, and 'girl power' helped make it seem more acceptable for women to be sexually more in charge. When it first became easily available on the net, porn seemed to seal the deal by becoming chic and daring for women to enjoy too. And, despite how far it had brought them, in the process feminism became seen as an old-fashioned concept that women didn't need any more – and which was shunned because it came to be associated with humourless man-hating.

But the fact we that we so quickly forgot how far we had come meant we took two steps forward, only to take one step back. In the last decade, sexual liberation has been neatly turned against our daughters so they believe they have to be slutty and man-pleasing to be sexy and that confidence means taking your clothes off.

In a straw poll of today's teenage girls for my last book, I found that most didn't have a clue what feminism was – or that it had ever been needed. But without it, how do our daughters know that their gender has a voice, that things can change – and that they don't have to fit into today's empty stereotypes if they don't want to?

The good news is that, as it has become clear how porn has led to a rise in harassment, misogyny and sexual violence, a new generation of young women activists are coming forward. The 'fourth wave' of feminism, led by movements like Everyday Sexism, is helping to wake girls and women up again. As I write, a new poll by GirlGuiding has found that three-quarters of teenage girls have woken up to see how sexism affects most areas of their lives, and believe there is 'overwhelming evidence of inequality for girls'. So, as your daughter gets older, encourage her to add her voice. Make the concept of equality simple and positive. There is no downside to everyone having equal rights. Make the word feminism interchangeable with the word equality.

To help your daughter check that equality is what she is getting, suggest she applies a simple litmus test. As Caitlin Moran suggests in *How to be a Woman*, ask 'are the boys worrying about or suffering from this too?'

Explain to your daughter that just as there was once racial apartheid in South Africa, there is still apartheid for women in some parts of the world. Tell her there are plenty of places in the world where girls are stopped from going to school, or where nine-year-old girls are married off by their families and are brutally punished if they leave the house or show their face in public. Question why in this country today, there is a still a national newspaper which features topless women among the news, as if women's breasts were as much public property as the weather and football results.

Just as racial equality is an ongoing topic of conversation in our society, get her to keep questioning if there is gender equality. Show her that while there are decent boys and men out there who want this too, it will only be achieved if more good men join the fight. The fact is that if your daughter sees her own struggles as part of a continuing campaign, she is less likely to be intimidated by her personal challenges – and more likely to feel angry enough to join others to do something about it. But if we say nothing and don't tell our girls that feminism is there for them, our daughters won't know how far they have come – or how far they still need to go.

WHAT YOU CAN DO

- **Don't let her hide her brains.** Girls have told me how classmates who get A*s across the board 'act dumb' because they think boys find 'airheads' sexier. I have stood in airport queues and seen teenage girls giggle because they think it's cute not to know where half the capital cities on the flight board are. Most girls will know the marital status of Angelina Jolie, but little about the humanitarian causes she espouses. Don't ever let your daughter think it's attractive to be ignorant.

- **Subscribe to a newspaper.** Our girls need to know what is happening in the world if they are to make up their minds about what to do about it. It's not as easy to share and discuss a newsfeed on an iPad as it is to sit around a newspaper. So, subscribe and keep one on the kitchen table as a point of discussion for the whole family.

- **Stimulate debate.** One of the most insidious effects of sexism is to make girls too self-conscious about their appearance to speak up. Encourage your daughter to talk about the issues of the day and encourage her to join the school debating club.

- **Form a mother-daughter book club.** One of the best ways to teach media literacy is a mother-daughter book club. The idea has been revived by educational psychologist, parenting coach and author of *Her Next Chapter*, Lori Day, who says these small groups show girls and mums how to push back against the messages around them. Lori says: 'It also helps mums find their voice, because even the culture for mums is pretty tough. Mothers face their own media assaults. It's hard not to feel intimidated or isolated when you're raising girls in this culture.'

I began this book by asking if it is still reasonable to expect our girls' childhoods to be uninterrupted by influences that would waylay their development. I posed the question: *Is it unrealistic in this day and age to believe our daughters shouldn't spend some of the most precious years of their lives worrying about adult concerns?*

Should we accept the fact that the carefree playtime that is so vital to our children's healthy emotional growth is going to be disturbed by anxieties about how they look as they play their games? Instead of enjoying wondering at their reflection in the mirror, should little girls' view of themselves already be beset by worries about conforming to the 'right' body shape and to ideals of beauty they never asked to be measured against? As our daughters grow, should the tentative process of getting to know boys romantically be derailed by the worry that they have to send naked pictures of themselves to be liked?

I could go on. Put like this, the answers to these questions are already obvious. Yet far too soon, parents have been led to believe that this is what modern childhood has become. All too quickly we have fallen into a state of helplessness, as if there were nothing to be done about the findings that we are raising the most anxious and depressed generation of girls ever recorded. Overwhelmed ourselves by the pace of change, instead we parents all too often find ourselves hoping our daughters will somehow dodge the curve balls being thrown at them – and miss out on the bruises they leave if they are not ready to receive them.

But, as I hope this book has shown, there are ways to train our girls how to catch those curve balls – and throw them right back. It doesn't have to be difficult. The skills needed to lob them back can be passed on in the ongoing dialogue you have with your daughter every day, whether it's while going to school, chatting at bedtime or eating a meal together. They can be taught in the moments when you help your daughter spot and reject those negative messages hurtling towards her that try to make her feel she is not good enough as she is. They can be developed when you really listen to her concerns so she does not turn them inwards, against herself, in her teenage years.

However fast the world moves, our girls need a childhood that is not disrupted by messages that interfere with their healthy development. So let's fight for girls' rights to grow in their own time, so they can grow deep roots as children – and then grow tall as adults. My daughters deserve an uninterrupted childhood. Never lose sight that yours do too.

SOURCES AND RESEARCH NOTES

Introduction

'There has been a 41 per cent increase in calls from children over the last year alone.' Source: 'Self-harm calls to ChildLine show biggest increase', Sean Coughlan, BBC News website, 5 December 2012 (based on ChildLine figures). Figures from the UK Department of Health also say up to 40 children a week were admitted to UK hospitals in 2014. The previous year, a record figure of 15,000 children under sixteen were seen by medical centres for intentional self-harm. To examine the overall trend in self-harm, look at the previous most comprehensive study of self-harm in England published by the *British Medical Journal* in 2002 (www.bmj.com/content/325/7374/1207). It surveyed around 6,000 fifteen- and sixteen-year-olds in 41 schools and found that 6.9 per cent of them said they had self-harmed over the past year. The 2013–14 WHO study now puts the figure at 20 per cent of fifteen-year-olds in the UK.

'One in ten children aged between five and sixteen now has a mental health issue.' Source: 'Mental health of children and adolescents in Great Britain', Office for National Statistics, 2000.

'One in four seven-year-old girls has tried to lose weight at least once and girls as young as five are worried about how they look and their size.' Source: 'Reflections on body image', All Party Parliamentary Group on Body Image and Central YMCA, 2012. The report also found that children and young people with body image dissatisfaction are less likely to engage in learning and participation in school.

'More than a quarter of children say they "often feel depressed" – and the thing that makes girls most unhappy is how they look.' Source: *A Good Childhood: Searching for Values in a Competitive Age*, Richard Layard and Judy Dunn (Penguin, 2009). The proportion of children aged eleven to fifteen who said they were relatively unhappy with their appearance had also risen from 10 per cent in 2002 to 14 per cent in 2012, according to an ONS study, 'Measuring national well-being, exploring the well-being of children in the UK, 2014'.

'By the time they are ten, 13 per cent of girls aged ten to seventeen would avoid giving an opinion.' Source: 'The real truth about beauty: revisited', Dove Global study, 2010. Base: 1,200 girls aged ten to seventeen in the USA, Canada, UK, Germany, Brazil and Russia.

PART ONE

Us as parents

'12 per cent of sixteen- to 21-year-olds would consider cosmetic surgery.' Source: 'Girls' attitudes survey', conducted by Childwise on behalf of Girlguiding, March 2012.

'Young people are the prime plastic surgery growth market.' Source: 'Cosmetic Surgery – UK – June 2010', report conducted by Mintel, 2010.

'The French Government has now moved to outlaw child beauty pageants.' Source: 'Putting a child in a French beauty pageant could lead to jail', Rory Mulholland, *Daily Telegraph*, 19 September 2013. Senators voted to outlaw such competitions and send parents to jail for up to two years if they tried to enter their children in mini pageants. This step was triggered by an inquiry into a *Vogue* photo shoot featuring ten-year-old Thylane Blondeau, photographed with heavy make-up.

'**More than 12,000 girls are entered into the Miss Teen Queen UK every year alone.**' Source: 'What are their mothers thinking?', Natasha Courtenay-Smith, *Daily Mail*, 30 May 2009.

'**Two out of three women have tried to lose weight in the past year.**' Source: A Mintel study cited in 'A record two in three women have dieted in past year, while 44% of men were among the 29 million Britons trying to slim', Sean Poulter, *Daily Mail*, 3 January 2014.

'**One in five parents feels they have little or no control over what their children see on the web anymore.**' Source: 'Bye buy childhood', Mother's Union report, September 2010.

'**By the time their children were fifteen, most parents believed it was "game over" and that kids were so tech-savvy they could no longer control their child's viewing.**' Source: 'Parents: We can't hold back the tide of porn on phones or computers', Paul Bentley and Laura Cox, *Daily Mail*, 14 January 2014. Researchers for the British Board of Film Classification questioned 10,000 people – including teenagers – about the viewing habits of young people, for a report to accompany revised guidance on film classification. The report said: 'Parents are working hard to maintain control, yet feel that the tide of information and challenging content can sometimes be against them.'

'**More than 250 studies have found that the best way to protect girls against early sexual behaviour is for them to be responsibly informed about sex in the first place.**' Source: 'Emerging answers: Research findings on programs to reduce teen pregnancy', Douglas Kirby, The National Campaign to Prevent Teen and Unplanned Pregnancy, May 2001 and November 2007.

Statistics on the number of children who have seen pornography. More than half of eleven- to fourteen-year-olds said they had seen online pornography, with four out of ten of those saying it had affected their relationships with others of their age, according to a poll of 2,000 youngsters aged eleven to 25 by the charity Young Minds, January 2014.

Parents don't realise when their children are watching porn.
Source: 'UK children go online', Sonia Livingstone and Magdalena Bober, LSE, 2007. 57 per cent of children between the ages of nine and nineteen have seen porn, but only 16 per cent of their parents knew.

The role of mothers
'At the age of eight, Poppy Burge is already following in her mum's footsteps.' Source: 'The mum "empowering" her daughter aged eight with £8,000 of beauty surgery', Andrew Dagnell, *Sunday Mirror*, 26 February 2012.

'Just 2 per cent of adult women feel they are beautiful.' Source: 'The real truth about beauty: Revisited', Dove, 2010.

The role of fathers
'A father may have even more of a role in building a girl's self-esteem than her mother.' Sources: 'The costs and benefits of active fatherhood: Evidence and insights to inform the development of policy and practice', Adrienne Burgess, the Fatherhood Institute, 2008. 'Fatherhood: Connecting the Strands of diversity across time and space', C. Lewis and M. Lamb, Report to the Joseph Rowntree Foundation, 2006.

'Daughters of men who put high importance on a woman's appearance were found to be much more likely to have made themselves sick to lose weight.' Source: 'Parental influences on the dieting beliefs and behaviors of adolescent females in New Zealand', Robyn Dixon, Vivienne Adair and Steven O'Connor, *Journal of Adolescent Health*, 19/4, October 1996.

'Hands-off dads may end up with more rebellious teen girls.'
Source: *Raising Confident Girls*, Ian and Mary Grant (Vermilion, 2009).

The role of schools

'The best way for schools and parents to work together is by creating an atmosphere where teachers and parents co-operate.'
Source: *So Sexy, So Soon*, Diane Levin (Ballantine Books, 2008).

'One in ten parents of girls going to proms said they have paid for their daughters to have spray tans.' Source: According to a OnePoll survey of 1,000 UK parents in June 2013, 13 per cent of parents pay for a manicure/pedicure, 10 per cent book a spray or fake tan and 10 per cent pay for professional make-up.

'This is all putting a lot of emphasis on image and looks at a very vulnerable point in their development.' Source: Author's interview with Chris Calland, educational consultant and co-author of *Body Image in the Primary School* (Routledge, 2011).

'Low-key celebrations – which involve parents – are a better idea for children this age.' Source: Author's interview with Russell Hobby, general secretary of the National Association of Head Teachers.

PART TWO

Self-worth

'How to create a growth mindset.' To find out more, go to http://mindsetonline.com/ or read Carol Dweck's book, *Mindset: How You Can Fulfil Your Potential* (Robinson, 2012).

'One in five seven- to fourteen-year-olds play outside for less than an hour a week.' Source: Survey by The Children's Society, cited in *A Good Childhood: Searching for Values in a Competitive Age*, Richard Layard and Judy Dunn (Penguin, 2009).

Connection and creating a sanctuary

'A total of 66 per cent of mothers now have jobs, compared with 23 per cent in 1971.' Source: Office for National Statistics, cited in 'More mothers working full-time', Louisa Peacock, *Daily Telegraph*, 31 March 2011.

Young children see being hurried by parents as a rejection. For more from Professor David Elkind on how children react to stress in the home, see his book, *The Hurried Child* (Da Capo Press, 2007).

'Half of parents now say they are too stressed and tired to read their kids a bedtime story.' Source: A survey by Raisingkids.co.uk polled 1,108 parents of children under the age of ten, and found that half said they were too tired to read to their children, and that work came first.

'A slower day is not coming.' Source: *The Sixty Minute Family: An Hour to Transform Your Relationships – Forever*, Rob Parsons (Lion Books, 2010).

Monitor your stress levels. For more, see *Fried:Why You Burn Out and How to Revive*, Joan Borysenko (Hay House, 2011).

'Researchers have found children get over an hour less sleep every night than they did a decade ago.' Source: According to a March 2014 poll by the National Sleep Foundation, more than half of fifteen- to seventeen-year-olds sleep about seven hours a night – 90 minutes less than the minimum recommendation – due to opportunities to socialise round the clock via technology.

'When UNICEF researchers asked children their requirements for happiness they named not only time with families and friends, but also time spent outdoors.' Source: 'Children's well-being in UK, Sweden and Spain: The role of inequality and materialism', Unicef, Ipsos Mori and Agnes Nairn, September 2011.

'**Apply the 80/20 rule.**' Source: *21st Century Girls: How the Modern World is Damaging Our Daughters and What We Can Do About It*, Sue Palmer (Orion, 2014).

Emotional intelligence
'**Traditional ways of measuring brainpower are much too narrow.**' For more, see *Frames of Mind: The Theory of Multiple Intelligences*, Howard Gardner (Basic Books, 2011) and *Emotional Intelligence: Why it Can Matter More Than IQ*, Daniel Goleman (Mass Market, 1996).

How to help your daughter find out who she is
'**Every child has a spark.**' For more, see Peter Benson's TEDx talk, 'Sparks: How youth thrive' at www.youtube.com/watch?v=TqzUHcW58Us

'**How to explain "social smarts" to kids and teaching them how to be social detectives.**' For more, see *You Are a Social Detective: Explaining Social Thinking to Kids*, Michelle Garcia Winner (North River Press, 2010).

'**Plotting a family tree helps make children feel grounded and part of something bigger.**' Source: According to a study published in Emory University's online *Journal of Family Life* in March 2010, family stories provide a sense of identity through time, and help children understand who they are in the world.

'**Help her to help others.**' Source: The Children's Society. Studies prove that unselfish people are happier than people who are preoccupied with themselves.

How to build communication
'**Making "emotional deposits".**' For more, see *7 Habits of Highly Effective Families*, Dr Stephen R. Covey (Simon & Schuster, 1999).

'**Hugging for just twenty seconds is enough to boost levels of the feel-good hormone oxytocin and keep kids up for the**

whole day.' Source: *Psychosomatic Medicine*, 67/4, August 2005. University of North Carolina researchers found that hugs increase the 'bonding' hormone oxytocin and cut the risk of heart disease. Furthermore, children who have high levels of oxytocin are savvier at communicating with others and interpreting social signals or situations, according to a study published by researchers at the Stanford University School of Medicine in the *Proceedings of the National Academy of Sciences*, 111/33, August 2014.

The importance of eating together. Sources: Just the act of joining family members at the table makes youngsters feel valued and has a positive effect on their emotional well-being, according to a study of 26,000 children aged between eleven and fifteen by psychiatrists at Canada's McGill University, published in the *Journal of Adolescent Health*, 52/3, March 2013. A 1994 *Reader's Digest* poll, 'What's behind success in school?', of 2,130 high school seniors also found that students who regularly shared meals with their families scored higher on academic tests than those who didn't. Of those who said their 'whole family sits around a table together for a meal' at least four times a week, 60 per cent got high scores, and their results rose with the number the times family ate together.

What to do if things go wrong
The rise of 'little miss perfect'. For more, see *The Curse of the Good Girl: Raising Authentic Girls with Courage and Confidence*, Rachel Simmons (Penguin, 2010).

Reconnecting with your child using 'love bombing'. For more, see *Love Bombing: Reset Your Child's Emotional Thermostat*, Oliver James (Karnac, 2012).

PART THREE
Pornography
Estimates on the number of children seeing porn. Source: 'Porn seen by a quarter of children under 12', Heather Saul, *Independent*,

10 April 2014. One in four young people have watched internet porn by the age of twelve or younger, according to a survey of 1,000 sixteen- to 21-year-olds, commissioned by the BBC for the documentary, *Porn: What's the harm?*

Most kids first see porn by accident. Source: Accidental exposure is discussed in a review of published evidence of 41,000 items of academic literature about pornography led by Middlesex University in partnership with the University of Bedfordshire, Canterbury Christ Church University and the University of Kent, supplemented by a focus group of young people, May 2013.

'A quarter of young people who saw porn initially first felt "disgust, shock or surprise".' Source: 'Inadvertent exposure to pornography on the Internet: Implications of peer-to-peer file-sharing networks for child development and families', Patricia M. Greenfield, *Applied Developmental Psychology*, 25, 2004.

The changing face of porn and why others may be frightened of raising the subject. Source: Author's interviews with Professor Gail Dines of Wheelock College, Boston.

Porn is the main source of sex education. Source: Opinion survey for the Institute for Public Policy Research, 2014. By the time teenagers reach their mid-teens, the internet was ranked higher than parents as a source of information about sex and relationships.

'90 per cent of the top rated porn sites these young men are looking at contain material portraying aggressive acts.' Source: September 2013 study by the University of East London of boys aged twelve to fifteen found that 97 per cent of those who had seen porn via a simple Google search were accessing scenes of staged rape, gagging and beating. The UEL survey, specially commissioned for the Channel 4 programme, *Porn on the Brain*, looked at teen porn habits and revealed some shocking results about the impact porn is having on young people's perception of sex and relationships today.

'The age of first exposure to porn is falling all the time, according to CEOP.' Source: See interviews in 'Clio is just seven. So why did her mother sit her down to warn her about internet porn?', Tanith Carey, *Daily Mail*, 6 June 2012.

How porn moves out of the cyber-world and into real life. Source: Rosa Silverman, *Daily Telegraph*, 19 November 2012. Primary school children as young as ten are being arrested over suspected rapes and other sexual offences. In 2011–12, 24 UK police forces arrested children under thirteen on suspicion of rape and seven detained at least one ten-year-old. According to a NSPCC spokesman, porn gives children 'a distorted picture of what sexual relationships should be about'.

The effect of porn on young people's sexual behaviour. Source: A May 2013 study by the Children's Commissioner for England also found a link between exposure to extreme images at a young age and a rise in 'risky behaviours'. Children who regularly viewed pornography were more likely to have underage sex, develop 'casual and hedonistic' attitudes, experiment with drink and drugs and sext. Boys were much more likely to be exposed to pornography than girls, leading to 'beliefs that women are sex objects'. The study, based on a large-scale review of international evidence, also found some evidence of a relationship between explicit images and a rise in sexual aggression and harassment of females.

In a 2014 poll by the Institute for Public Policy Research, more than seven out of ten girls said porn had pressured them to look and act differently. Another report, 'A rapid evidence assessment on the effects that access and exposure to pornography has on children and young people', by the Office of the Children's

Commissioner, found that a significant number of children said porn influenced their attitudes towards relationships and sex.

'Depression in teenage girls may often be "a sexually transmitted disease".' Source: *Your Kids at Risk: How Teen Sex Threatens Our Sons and Daughters*, Dr Meg Meeker (Regnery Publishing, 2007).

'Psychologists are asking what it means for future generations when the young addicts that are sent to them for counselling have viewed porn from such a young age.' For more, see the author's interview with John Woods, consultant psychotherapist at the Portman Clinic, London: 'Jamie is thirteen and hasn't even kissed a girl. But he's now on the Sex Offender Register after online porn warped his mind', *Daily Mail*, 26 April 2012.

'It's not adults who say porn is ruining our children's childhoods, it's young people themselves.' Source: Opinium survey for the Institute for Public Policy Research (IPPR), August 2014. Eight out of ten eighteen-year-olds say it's far too easy to accidentally view explicit images, and seven out of ten said their childhood would have been better if porn had not been so available.

'More than one in five women feel the need to do more in bed to maintain their partner's interest, with one in seven feeling pressured to play out scenes that their partner has viewed on X-rated websites.' Source: *Pornified: How Pornography is Damaging Our Lives, Our Relationships, and Our Families*, Pamela Paul (Owl, 2006).

'The real reason that teen pregnancy rates are falling in this country.' Source: According to the Office of National Statistics, the under-eighteen conception rate fell in 2012 to 27.9 per cent, the lowest figure since records began in 1969. There were 27,834 pregnancies among under-eighteens in England and Wales in 2012 – down by around 10 per cent from the 31,051 in 2011.

'**Sex education does not speed up interest in sex.**' Source: 'Emerging answers: Research findings on programs to reduce teen pregnancy', Douglas Kirby, The National Campaign to Prevent Teen and Unplanned Pregnancy, May 2001 and November 2007. Studies from around the world have found that sex education by parents at an appropriate pace from an early age delays the timing of first sexual encounters.

Pop videos

Sexual content in pop videos. Source: 'MTV smut peddlers: Targeting kids with sex, drugs and alcohol', an investigation into MTV's content by the Parents' Television Council in 2004 found it contained 1,548 sexual scenes with 3,056 depictions of sex or nudity in 171 hours. Commenting on the findings, Dr Jane Brown, journalism professor at the University of North Carolina, Chapel Hill, said: 'If you believe *Sesame Street* taught your four-year-old something, then you better believe MTV is teaching your fourteen-year-old something, because the influence doesn't stop when we come to a certain age.'

Kids copying lyrics and provocative dance moves. Source: A November 2013 Netmums poll of 1,500 parents found that more than eight out of ten said that their child had sung or repeated sexual song lyrics.

Pretty babies

Make-up use among young girls is rising. Source: A study of nearly 1,300 girls aged seven to 21 by Girlguiding UK, cited in '"Growing number of girls suffer low self-esteem", says report. "More girls now unhappy with the way they look while sexual harassment is commonplace"', James Meikle, *Guardian*, 29 November 2013. According to the survey nearly two-thirds of seven- to eleven-year-olds use nail polish, half wear make-up and one-third wear high heels, although they see this as just 'being a girl' rather than as trying look older. See also 'Trends in tween cosmetics', Samantha Rose, fashionindustrytoday.com, 2 May 2008 and 'Graduating from Lip Smackers', Douglas Quenqua, New York Times, 29 April 2010, citing market research by NPD.

'27 per cent of girls feel under pressure to look beautiful by the time they are eleven.' Source: A report based on face-to-face interviews with 500 girls between eleven and seventeen from across Britain, from the April 2012 Dove Self-Esteem Project. It also found that Britain could lose some 319,000 future businesswomen, lawyers and doctors, as well as more than 60 women MPs, by 2050 unless young women can be helped to retain confidence in their own abilities. Cited in 'Girls' lack of confidence about their appearance is blighting their futures', Luke Salkeld, Daily Mail, 1 April 2012.

'Half of three- to six-year-old girls say they worry about being fat, according to the British Journal of Developmental Psychology.' Source: Girls begin worrying about their appearance and weight from the age of three, according to a study in the British Journal of Developmental Psychology: 'Am I too fat to be a princess?: Examining the effects of popular children's media on young girls' body image', Sharon Hayes and Stacey Tantleff-Dunn, June 2010. Researchers at the University of Central Florida asked a group of girls aged between three and six a series of questions about their body image before showing them extracts of cartoons featuring female characters. Almost a third – 31 per cent – said that they 'almost always' worried about their appearance, while another 18 per cent said that they sometimes did so. Thirty per cent of the children said they would like to change at least one physical attribute.

Body image
'By the age of ten, one in ten girls is "extremely worried" about becoming fat and one in four has tried dieting.' Source: 'Frequency and patterns of eating disorder symptoms in early adolescence', National Institute for Health Research, December

2013. A study of 7,000 teenagers found that two-thirds of thirteen-year-old girls are afraid of gaining weight and over half are avoiding certain foods to stop themselves getting fat. By the age of seven, 70 per cent of seven-year-olds want to be thinner. By nine, nearly half have been on a diet. For more, see the study above, 'Am I too fat to be a princess?'.

The effect of a mother's body image on her daughter. Source: The author's interview with Deanne Jade, founder of the National Centre for Eating Disorders, eating-disorders.org.uk.

'The average adult woman thinks negatively about her body image 36 times a day.' Source: In a November 2009 experiment for London Tonight, more than 100 women aged between 35 and 70 were asked to spend a week carrying a special click device which they had to press each time they had a negative thought about their face, body or themselves in general. On average, the women clicked their device 36 times every day – adding up to an average total of 252 negative thoughts in a week.

'Mature, adult women never ever give themselves a break from dieting.' Source: An online survey as part of the Gender and Body Image Study (GABI), published in *The International Journal of Eating Disorders*, found that there is no upper age limit on disordered eating. See also *Midlife Eating Disorders: Your Journey to Recovery*, Dr Cynthia M. Bulik (Walker Books, 2013).

The steep rise in the number of pre-teen children treated for anorexia and other eating disorders. Source: Global Burden of Disease study published in *The Lancet*, May 2014. According to NHS figures, hospital admissions have tripled for eating disorders in the last four years, while 29 per cent of UK girls are classed as overweight or obese.

'Seven out of ten overweight eleven-year-olds go on to become obese young adults.' Source: 'Childhood obesity, prevalence and prevention', Mahshid Dehghan, Noori Akhtar-Danesh and Anwar T. Merchant, *Nutrition Journal*, April 2005.

PMT may be all in the mind. Source: A study by the University of Otago in New Zealand, published in the journal *Gender Medicine*, cited in 'Premenstrual syndrome may be a myth', Lucy Kinder, *Daily Telegraph*, 25 October 2012. The study analysed 47 studies dating from 1971 to 2007 and looked for evidence for mood swings in the days before a woman's period. Only 15 per cent of the studies found signs of this happening.

Branded

'By the time they're seventeen, girls have seen 250,000 TV commercials.' Source: 'The impact of exposure to the thin-ideal media image on women' by Nicole Hawkins, P. Scott Richards, H. Mac Granley and David M. Stein, published in *Eating Disorders*, 12/1, Spring 2004. Women on TV and in magazines are on average 15 per cent thinner than the average woman, and the advent of Photoshop means that 99 per cent of magazine pictures have now been digitally altered.

The rise of the selfie. Source: 91 per cent of teenagers have posted selfies online, according to the Pew Center for Internet Research. See 'Teens, social media, and privacy', May 2013.

'The self-esteem of girls who spend a lot of time on Facebook is likely to be damaged.' Source: 'Heavy web use harms a child's mental health: Every hour raises risk, warns watchdog', Daniel Martin, *Daily Mail*, 16 May 2014. Public Health England, which issues guidance on good health to the NHS, says there is a clear relationship between the amount of time spent on social media sites such as Facebook and 'lower levels of well-being'. The link becomes particularly striking when children spend more than four hours a day in front of a screen – but it kicks in even at very low levels of use.

Self-harm

Self-harm is rising. Source: 'Thousands of children treated for self-harm including three-year-old who deliberately overdosed on paracetamol', Hugo Gye, *Daily Mail*, 20 May 2014. More than 12,644 young people were admitted to hospital after self-harming in 2013, according to figures obtained in a series of Freedom of Information requests. Because a quarter of NHS trusts did not respond, the true number is likely to be higher. In 2012, fewer than 10,000 children were found to have self-harmed, meaning the number has soared by nearly 30 per cent.

'How to talk to children about self-harm when they are young.' Source: Author's interview with Rachel Welch, director of selfharm.co.uk. For further reading see: 'Teenagers who cut themselves are too often dismissed as looking for attention. But their distress is real, and their numbers are growing', Kate Hilpern, *Independent*, 13 October 2013.

'A study of more than 600 first-year university students found that 9 per cent had posted toxic remarks about themselves.' Source: 'The teens who troll themselves: In a shocking new form of self-harming, some young people have become their own vile online bullies', Tanith Carey, *Daily Mail*, 26 February 2014.

'Children are cyber-bullying themselves.' Source: An investigation into cyber-bullying cases by an online question-and-answer network, Form Spring, now renamed Spring Me, also hit an obstacle when it was found that many of the bullying attacks were by the 'victims' themselves.

Connected

'Youngsters are increasingly showing signs of compulsion in their use of tablets and smartphones.' Source: A May 2014 survey by Tablets for Schools questioned more than 2,000 secondary school pupils aged between eleven and seventeen and found that as many as four in ten teenagers believe they are addicted to the internet. The figure was higher among girls at 46 per cent, whereas 36 per cent of boys thought they were addicted.

'Children who regularly play games like Angry Birds or Fruit Ninja had lower scores in speech tests for both understanding language and speaking.' Source: A May 2013 study of 65 families by the Cohen Children's Medical Center of New York.

Friendships

Friendship makes children's childhoods happiest. Source: *A Good Childhood: Searching for Values in a Competitive Age*, Layard and Dunn (Penguin, 2009).

Creative play is important to forming friendships. Source: A study by psychologist John Gottman found that creative imaginative play is the core feature of friendship – but that it quickly stops once parents burst the play bubble. See *Raising An Emotionally Intelligent Child*, John Gottman and Joan DeClaire (Prentice Hall, 1998).

'Don't use the silent treatment.' Source: 'Aversive parenting in China: Associations with child physical and relational aggression', David Nelson, *Child Development*, 77/3, May/June 2006.

'No matter what they do to her, a girl still feels her friends know her best and want what is best for her.' Source: *Queen Bees and Wannabes*, Rosalind Wiseman (Three Rivers Press, 2002).

Wired children

'By the age of nine, a quarter of children are on social networks.' Source: Social Networking and Privacy Report, UK Council for Child Internet Safety, April 2011.

'Explicit webcam use involving children is rising.' Source: 'Children of twelve exposed to explicit conversations on webcam chat sites', Lucy Osbourne, *Daily Mail*, 30 March 2013.

Children as young as twelve see obscene images and have explicit conversations on free video chat websites, according to the Child Exploitation and Online Protection Centre. Up to 50 per cent of the live video streams on these websites contain nudity or graphic acts, in particular involving men. CEOP described the websites' effect on young people as 'devastating'.

'The sexier girls look in their profile pictures, the more likely they are to be targeted by adult predators.' Source: 'Key children's sites adopt click CEOP button as UK's Centre for Child Protection receives over 6,000 reports in a year', www.ceop.police.uk/Media-Centre/Press-releases/2010/, 5 November 2010.

Television
Verbal aggression in reality TV programmes. Source: A study by researchers at Brigham Young University, USA, published in the *Journal of Broadcasting and Electronic Media*, Professor David Nelson, June 2010.

Effects of media on body image. Source: Reflections on Body Image report, All Party Parliamentary Group on Body Image, May 2012. The main perceived social influences on body image were the media (43.5 per cent), advertising (16.8 per cent) and celebrity culture (12.5 per cent).

'Fewer than 5 per cent of the population could ever attain the current body ideals being portrayed.' Source: As above.

'Girls who watch reality TV are more focussed on physical appearance.' Source: As above.

Fashion
Kids' luxury wear valued at 6.5 billion. Source: 'Child models gear up for the first Global Kids Fashion Week in London', Daisy Bridgewater, *Daily Telegraph*, 9 March 2013.

'Children recognise logos from the age of eighteen months.'
Source: BRANDchild: *Remarkable insights in the minds of today's global kids and their relationships with brands*, Martin Lindstrom (Kogan Page, 2003).

Girls turned off sports by ugly kits. Source: 2014 research carried out by Virgin Active found that 39 per cent of girls, rising to 46 per cent among sixteen-year-olds, say they enjoy being active but hate the PE kit.

Material girls

'58 per cent of nine to fourteen-year-olds buy stuff to belong.'
Source: 'Peer pressures and poverty', Richard Elliott and Claire Leonard, *Journal of Consumer Behaviour*, 3/4, 2004.

'Teenage children have gadgets worth over £5,000.' Source: Online research survey commissioned by Esure via Onepoll, which interviewed a random sample of 3,000 UK parents, December 2009.

Toys

'Girls who play with Barbies have a worse body image and a narrower outlook after playing with them.' Source: 'Effect of Barbie play on girls' career cognitions', *Sex Roles*, March 2014. A study by psychology professors Aurora Sherman of Oregon State and Eileen Zurbriggen at UC Santa Cruz found that girls who play with Barbie dolls tend to see fewer career options available to them compared with the options available to boys.

Engaged

'21 per cent of children of four can find their way around a smartphone but only 14 per cent can tie their own shoelaces.'
Source: 'Generation HELPLESS: Children are now better at using smartphones than swimming, tying their shoelaces and even telling the time', *Daily Mail*, 9 September 2014. According to a study that surveyed 2,000 parents of children aged between two

and sixteen in the UK, more than half of children aged between two and ten feel more confident using a tablet than learning to swim, telling the time and tying their shoe laces. The majority of young children also said they felt more confident using a mobile phone than reading.

The number of children sexting is on the rise. Source: According to a six-year study by researchers at the University of Texas Medical Branch at Galveston which looked at the sexting habits of more than 1,000 secondary school students, sexting among teenagers is becoming a 'normal' part of growing up. It found that a third of under-eighteens have been affected by sexting, and girls as young as eleven are frequently asked to send intimate photos to boys they know. The NSPCC in the UK found that there was a 28 per cent increase in calls that mentioned sexting to ChildLine in 2012–13, compared to the previous year, and a 2012 NSPCC study also found that 40 per cent of young people had taken part in sexting and suggested that girls were under huge pressure to join in the craze.

Harassment, misogyny and abuse
'One in four twelve-year-olds has dealt with street harassment.' Source: A study by Stop Street Harassment (www.stopstreetharassment.org) found that one in four twelve-year-olds and 90 per cent of nineteen-year-olds had experienced harassment.

FURTHER READING

Aldort, Naomi, *Raising Our Children, Raising Ourselves*, Book Publishers Network, 2006

Bates, Laura, *Everyday Sexism*, Simon & Schuster UK, 2014

Benn, Melissa, *What Shall We Tell Our Daughters?* Hodder, 2013

Berman, Laura, *Sex Ed.*, Dorling Kindersley, 2009

Borysenko, Joan, *Fried: Why you burn out and how to revive*, Hay House, 2011

Carey, Tanith, *Taming the Tiger Parent: How to put your child's well-being first in a competitive world*, Robinson, 2014

Chachamu, Miriam, *How to Calm a Challenging Child*, Foulsham, 2008

Craven, Pat, *Living with the Dominator*, Freedom Publishing, 2008

Day, Lori and Kugler, Charlotte, *Her Next Chapter: How mother-daughter book clubs can help girls navigate malicious media, risky relationships, girl gossip and so much more*, Chicago Review Press, 2014

Deak, Joanne, *Raising Confident and Courageous Daughters*, Hyperion, 2002

Dines, Gail, *Pornland*, Beacon Press, 2010

Durham, MG, *The Lolita Effect*, Gerald Duckworth & Co, 2009

Dweck, Carol, *Mindset: How you can fulfil your potential*, Robinson, 2012

Gardner, Howard, *Frames of Mind*, Basic Books, 2011

Goleman, Daniel, *Emotional Intelligence*, Bloomsbury, 1996

Grant, Ian and Grant, Mary, *Raising Confident, Girls*, Vermilion, 2009

Hamilton, Maggie, *What's Happening to our Girls?* Viking, 2008

Hughes-Joshi, Liat, *How to Unplug Your Child*, Vie, 2015

James, Oliver, *Love Bombing: Reset your child's emotional thermostat*, Karnac Books, 2012

James, Oliver, *They F*** You Up: How to survive family life*, Bloomsbury, 2006

Janis-Norton, Noël, *Calmer, Easier, Happier Parenting: The revolutionary programme that transforms family life*, Hodder & Stoughton, 2012. For courses from Noël, go to www.tnlc.info

Layard, Richard and Dunn, Judy, *A Good Childhood: Searching for values in a competitive age*, Penguin, 2009

Levin, Diane, *So Sexy So Soon*, Ballantine Books, 2008

Maisel, Gail, *Feelings can be friends*, Panoma Press, 2013

Palmer, Sue, *Toxic Childhood: How the modern world is damaging our children and what we can do about it*, Orion, 2007

Palmer, Sue, *21st Century Girls*, Orion, 2013

Parsons, Rob, *The Sixty Minute Family*, Lion, 2010

Richards, Naomi, *The Parent's Toolkit: Simple and effective ways to help your child be their best*, Vermilion, 2012

Said, Carole and Nadim, *Kids Don't Come with a Manual*, Best of parenting publications, 2015

Simmons, Rachel, *Curse of the Good Girl*, Penguin, 2010

Wiseman, Rosalind, *Queen Bees and Wannabes: Helping your daughter survive cliques, gossip, boyfriends & the new realities of Girl World*, Piatkus, 2003

ACKNOWLEDGEMENTS

With many thanks to all the following, as well as the many mums and daughters who shared their experiences with me:

Noël Janis-Norton at the New Learning Centre, Michelle Garcia Winner, Kate Kirkpatrick, Deanne Jade, Professor Julia Buckroyd, Sonia Ducie, Natalie Collins, Anthony Harwood, Lily and Clio Harwood, Professor Gail Dines, Dr Linda Papadopoulous, Caroline Montgomery, Kate Hewson at Icon, Rachel Welch at selfharm.co.uk, Philip Hodson, Carole and Nadim Said at www.bestofparenting.co.uk, Dr Nollaig Frost, Pippa Smith and Miranda Suit of Safermedia, Bethany Becconsall, Lori Day and John Woods.

INDEX